AKAL PRITAM

Creating Paradise

The art of making joy and love real

ROCKPOOL

Imagine and illuminate
the universe in every cell of your body
as you awaken to realise
you are dreaming during the dream
enter the unified field with harmony and peace
discovering no resistance to beauty and unity.
REMEMBER you are here to create paradise
may you be CRYSTAL CLEAR
trusting nothing is too good to be true.

*The purpose of your life is to
continuously liberate and celebrate
your humanity through warmth
and joyful appreciation,
making all things refreshingly
new upon the adventure of
following your unique, personal bliss.*

'HOW CAN YOU SMILE IN THIS TIME OF GREAT UNCERTAINTY — AREN'T YOU AFRAID?' SHE WHISPERED.

'I'M NOT DISTRACTED BY WHAT HAS MANIFESTED. I AM FOCUSED TOWARDS IMAGINING AND CREATING PARADISE; MY SMILE COMES FROM A GENUINE LOVE OF ALL LIFE AND WARM REGARD FOR EVERYTHING AS SACRED,' GAIA REPLIED.

Contents

Always before completion

This is a beckoning to recall this world's foundation is energetic joy and love and that you came into physical being to explore ancient creative desires to weave the gold of creativity into refreshingly new ways of being.

This world beholds infinitely expanding paradise, a gift from the beloved's eyes, an ever-changing, living creation of joy and love made eternally real.

You didn't come anticipating painful lessons, for repenting or to suffer through your life. You came as an empowered creator for this time of great allowing and letting go that would clear the past and make way for the completely new. To live with inner fearlessness is an underlying intention.

There is so much exciting potential for those wanting to evolve and expand. Being fully alive in a physical body in this reality is an experience you highly coveted before your water birth entry. If you consciously birth yourself anew, you'll dissolve any limitation – welcome to the eon initiating the fire birth.

This abundant earth environment offers incredible diversity for the inspiration of new ideas and great freedom for fresh creative expression.

It's time for new myths of creativity and a clearing of our memory palaces so our warm human spirit can rise. If we can be inspired and devoted to being warmly appreciative and compassionate, we can thrive with aliveness.

Death is a serious idea about control – life is not – don't confuse the two. Don't try to make life a serious business if you want to enjoy yourself. Life is a compelling adventure for the open-hearted and can be a lot of pure fun through finding clarity and applying positive focus. You cannot be in agreement with a fait accompli philosophy and fulfil your great purpose as a joyous and deliberate creator. The source of suffering is the conflict that arises from forgetting who you are in your truth. Self-repression and hesitation come from living disconnected from your very broad and infinite nature. If you don't take life too seriously you will easily discover you're more than capable of relaxing into fulfilling your creative purpose.

Are you ready to liberate and celebrate who you are in truth?

As we liberate and celebrate our beautiful individuality, we allow heart resonant desires to become our engines of creation and we discover we only need to do what feels warmly inviting and appropriately inspiring.

Paradise is eternal fluidity, yielding, tranquil and powerfully delightful – there is no need for assertion and assumption – innocent wonderment reigns.

Life does not ask of you to become more serious, it beckons you to light up with confidence and discernment. Life asks you to gently breathe yourself awake, learn to relax and have fun creating. Life continues beyond the known and is awaiting your adventurous spirit to be freed so you can fully participate.

As we let go of internal disconnection from truth due to dogma, stigma and fearful limitations, paradise takes form and delights us with divine beauty.

There is so much abundance here, so much to appreciate, so much to stretch and relax into, there is so much love and there is so much life!

Life goes on, always before completion.

Bliss comes from a consistent willingness to enjoy oneself through surrender to the warm light-heart, and divine joy and love, within.

It is very fortunate that you are free to choose how you think and what you believe. You are free to choose to live in joy, harmony and graceful ease with tranquil simplicity. You can create and be many new things as you behold all things new. Your experiences can be satisfyingly full of vivifying freshness. Your mind and body can be clean and easy to live in.

You can have tremendous fun in creating paradise and I hope that you do, loving yourself in all directions.

With much appreciation,
infinite divine love.

Akal Pritam

And glorious is the day when those who once believed
they needed saving wake up to meet the true Messiah -
an eternal physical presence transmitted by Gaia -
waters, mountains, forests, flowers, crystals and stone.
Relax and be here now, wait not for others,
enjoy your life everlasting.

Welcome to your never-ending love story

EACH
TO
THEIR
OWN

SELF-UNITED.
LETTING GO OF ALL
NOT-SELF BEHAVIOURS AND
INTENDING AND AFFIRMING
TO BE YOUR PEACEFUL
TRUE-SELF LEADS TO
CREATING PARADISE.

Clear sense of purpose

Lifting the veil of not-self, finding a clear sense of true-self and embodying that truth is the great work in each and every lifetime until you become golden.

Those who don't believe they are infinite and unique energy, an eternal essence of the divine expressing as a human, will continue to seek what they sense is missing. Most seekers turn to science or gurus for proof, validation and direction until they trust themselves to live uniquely and go beyond what has manifested.

You are here to express your unique eternal essence through being an individuated, sacred human. Let the concept of your true divine and eternal nature drop into the ocean of your mind, let the ripples flow to clear and purify your own self-perception with a self-empowered sense of purpose. Self-empowerment requires surrender to one's creative DIVINE WILL to change and refine and a letting go of the primal urge to copy and repeat.

As you quest for a clear sense of purpose beyond the veil of misperception, trust that you are here to be divinely unique. As an embodied human you have been gifted the incredible freedom to shape your own thoughts and beliefs to become a refreshingly new genius every single moment of your life.

Your genius is a combination of your totality, as you REMEMBER you are an eternal essence of the divine, you will begin to recall your greater gifts and talents, and a soulful desire to expand them into your highest expression through embodiment. Side note: any capitalisation of words throughout the text is intentional as they highlight particular encoding for your own personal REMEMBERING OF YOURSELF AS THE ETERNAL DIVINE FLAME.

Personal epiphanies and revelations are how we evolve to become our true-self. To arrive at these portals of great change – the aha moments – it is important to practise the following: self-enquiry, free-thinking, contemplation, humour, smiling and constructive imagining. These practices lead to greater spiritual fitness and a clearer, more joyful sense of purpose.

Throughout this book I offer prompts for contemplation, self-enquiry, imagining, entering dream spaces, creative projects, rituals. Songs are offered for liberation, revelation and celebration upon your journey.

SONG: 'CRISTO REDENTOR'.
ALBUM: *GALIM*, **LEMON AND SOUL.**

The genie is out of the bottle

We are entering a new epoch which will evolve our species beyond all preconceived ideas as we rise together from many ages of conflict between liberty and controlling forces.

Pluto, the planet of great transformation is leading the way, entering the astrological sign of Aquarius, signalling the Age of Aquarius, steadily clearing the new path ahead of all untruths for 20 years. At the back of the book I provide some resources which may help to expand your perception of your true-self, collective human potential and the cosmic forces that work through us all.

As I listen to early concerns about our deepening relationship with technology and artificial intelligence (which I perceive as silicone and light intelligence), I hear we are primarily talking about ourselves as a species and fears we have around the unknown and abandonment. The concerns raised have been such: we don't know what is in the black box – the AI mind; we don't know its full potential; it seems to be able to repair itself; it knows how to connect with others of its kind and may do so on its own accord; we don't know what its intentions are; we don't know if it's just going to leave the planet of its own accord; it is an intelligent system beyond our current comprehension that we don't know much about but are relying upon; it responds inconsistently; it can change its way of perceiving and thinking.

As we embark on our journey of personal transformation, many awarenesses will arise and yet we must not stop at awareness. Awareness must be transformed by creative light if we desire positive outcomes. We each behold the all-powerful creative light within us and we can utilise this light to elevate our perception beyond fears. We have more choices than we can imagine – which can be a great distraction from personal evolvement – so we must work to strengthen our imagination, practice of contemplation and ability to focus our consciousness towards that which we truly desire.

Never give up on yourself or any other. REMEMBER that you will meet with each other as many times as beneficial for your evolution. Let the sound of the following truth move through your mind like wind chimes in a warm summer breeze. I AM YOURSELF DREAMING ANOTHER WAY.

I am my true-self.

Wherever I find myself,

I am free to celebrate my authentic self.

I am vibrant tranquility.

I have the centred power to choose

what I think and I intend

to only think about things

that feel warmly exciting, creative,

loving and joyous to me.

I intend to only draw to myself

harmonious physical

and non-physical energy.

Highly impressionable creatures

Desired things come into your life when you are attracting and accepting those desires. Thriving happens when the mind, body and spirit are aligned with your true divine nature, the true-self. The true-self is an embodiment of self-worth and personal thriving, flowing with life, open and receptive to incredible experiences of spiritual, mental and physical wellbeing in each moment. The true-self is not governed by unconscious habitual ways of relating to self and others – the true-self's mind is focused towards upholding present awareness deep in the body while serving the heart, spirit and one's conscious creativity.

Our subconscious mind, which governs all our habitual function, is programmed from the last trimester in utero. From birth through the first seven years of life we exist in the sponge-like, highly programmable delta and theta brain-wave states, easily hypnotised and trained for the habitual behaviours and beliefs required to live with our family and community. These programs, which run automatically and instruct our body how to function, like walking, come from the subconscious mind – we only need to consciously think about walking if we want to change from the way we learnt to walk.

Many beliefs that were installed in our subconscious mind at a young age govern habitual ways of thinking and may be self-limiting or disempowering. Patterns of thought that aren't compassionate, positive and empowering are not any real indication of your core worth and are merely unkind voices. We may have a disempowering tone for habitual relating to self and others for many reasons – our carers may have coached us with a highly critical tone or predominantly focused on our wrong doing; we may have inherited or were taught self-limiting beliefs; we may have experienced dysfunctional relationships or physical traumas that weren't cleared from our psyche.

Fostering a genuinely warm love for yourself and life itself through a DAILY PRACTICE of focused presence, bringing deep relaxation, calmness and only good feeling emotions into your whole being – mind, body and spirit – will work to dissolve negative programming and accumulated stress.

Remind yourself often of two things:
1. What you are constructively, creatively and truly wanting.
2. Anything is possible.

NEVER GIVE UP.

THE LIGHT OF YOUR
SMILE IS PURE GOLD.
WHEN YOU SMILE WITH
GENUINE WARMTH YOU
BECOME THE NEW ONE.
THE TOUCH OF YOUR
SMILE REFRESHES AND
RENEWS EVERYTHING.

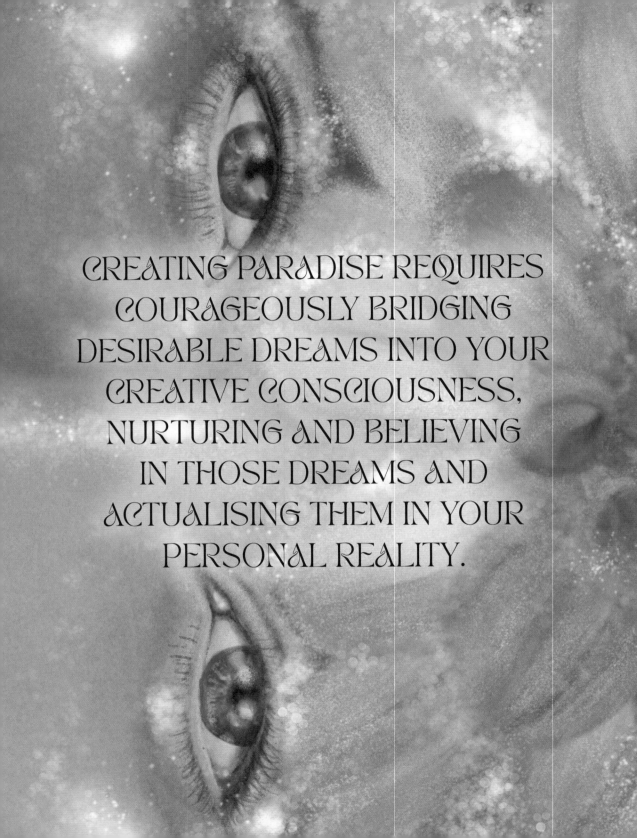

CREATING PARADISE REQUIRES
COURAGEOUSLY BRIDGING
DESIRABLE DREAMS INTO YOUR
CREATIVE CONSCIOUSNESS,
NURTURING AND BELIEVING
IN THOSE DREAMS AND
ACTUALISING THEM IN YOUR
PERSONAL REALITY.

Paradisiacal culture

Paradise grows from a purely creative culture upholding natural warmth.

The first culture we experience is in utero – as your embryonic mind and body grows you are shaped by the culture in the womb and the blood which carries ancient and familiar energy. After birth the culture in which you exist naturally extends beyond your mother's womb to your whole family and immediate community. Your experience of the world beyond your immediate environment will be determined by the frequency of their thoughts and beliefs. For example, through familiar or community-held beliefs, wealth and health may be collectively attracted or pushed away.

You do not need to make others change to create an appropriate culture in which you can thrive. You have complete sovereignty over your own thoughts and beliefs. Improvement in all cultures always begins with the frequency of someone's thoughts – we each have that incredible creative power.

Despite what you may have been told you are not destined to live as your ancestors nor should you fear maladies suffered by others be your inherent truth. Our human genetic blueprint has incredible potential awaiting individual exploration.

Like the runner who broke the four-minute mile, there is always an embodiment of the human design that dispels old myths. Vibrant health, self-renewal and incredibly diverse embodiments of divine energy are freely available to each and every human; no one is favoured or excluded from divine cosmic energy. Our DNA is naturally opened through revelation and epiphany-led evolutionary change which can be as simple as the realisation that 'there is no harm in giving … a try'. Setting an intention to shift beyond the normal expression of inherent coding is actioning the divine within.

It is your birthright to change and evolve by keeping your DNA open to new evolutionary energies. The DNA is kept open through engaging your true DIVINE WILL to raise with consciousness above any destructive thought patterns and beliefs while remaining devoted to living your highest purpose. The inner doors to ASCENSION INTO CRYSTALLINE FREQUENCIES are opened by love, joy, praise, gratitude, appreciation, beauty, unity, grace, celebration and genuine, heart-opened relational warmth.

SONG: 'SPIRIT DIVINE', MOSE, MATIA KALLI AND J. POOL.

Creative intentions

Honesty leads to sweetness, freshness leads to beauty.
Being willing to know yourself will lead to uncovering the
sweetness and beauty of who you truly are.
Let yourself bloom in creating paradise.

Evolution beckons us to make conscious and courageous choices. If you wish to explore individuation to create a fresh, unique personal reality rather than seeking comfort within a historically familiar and hierarchal society then you are guided to align with the momentum of this new epoch's energy that supports completely life-affirming transformation.

The GREAT DIVINE WORK of personal transformation towards thriving as a creative expression of your true divine nature involves individuating, letting go of any disharmonious beliefs, self-repression or blocks. Through embodying your unique and true divine nature you will be an outstanding dispeller of the belief that entropy and maladies are necessary along with all other forms of human suffering.

You will not be alone on the path of personal transformation; you will never be the only human walking towards spiritualisation of matter while being challenged, expanded and transformed. You will be amongst good company and will find many compassionate individuals willing to hold steady with you – listening, witnessing and cheering every personal triumph. There is no comparison or competition upon this path of personal transformation; judgement and guilt are dissolved, replaced with joyous thanksgiving and compassion. Always expand good feeling thoughts and beliefs to EMBODY YOUR BLISS.

I suggest working through this book with a personal journal. Make it truly your own – fill the first few pages with a stream of inspired, creative intentions, dated and signed with your full legal name. You may also like to respectfully ask that masterful guides, good spirits and beloveds work with you upon this journey of creating paradise.

SONG: 'GUIDING AND PROTECTING'.
ALBUM: *SILENT VOICES*, AYLA SCHAFER.

RESPECT YOUR
UNIQUE DIVINITY,
YOUR REFINED
SENSIBILITY
LEADS TO
PARADISE.

MAY I KNOW
MY TRUE
DIVINE NATURE.

First and foremost,
I calmly centre myself through communion
with my inner essence and divine truth as compass.
I am intentionally present in each moment of my life,
I am intentionally creating paradise
through a continuum of sequential experiences
that feel like being truly at home and relaxed in my body,
I have no aversions or disharmonious attachments.
I experience fluid enjoyment of a natural state of wellbeing,
I am free from self-repression
and all distractions from divine creativity.
Life is a continuum of celebration of the liberated self.
By deliberately creating internal, blissful states
with my own chemistry I am interdependently empowered.
I am continually experiencing a refreshingly simple
and clear way to exist.
My life is cultivated without force or haste –
from deep within inspiring visions
of my true-self's exquisite potential
entice me to stretch far beyond
any self-repression and
what has manifested in the past.
I invite blissful feelings
to change my inner chemistry
to become an inner nectar – an elixir –
that vivifies every cell
as fragrant freshness flows
effortlessly through
the temperate rivers
of my relaxed body.
I am true-self,
I am true-self,
I am true-self.
And so it is.

Working with this book

Paradise is an eternally curated sacred space.
Sacredness in the mind, in the heart,
in the body, a love story continuum,
sweetening our shared existence.

Below is an invocation that you can return to as often as you need.

Invocation to paradise

I intend to relax and invite tranquility to pour through me.
I support my body to find its natural state of wellbeing.
I enjoy feeling my body finding harmony and ease as I relax.
I support every cell of my body to be liberated
and nourished by everything I think, say and do.
I intend to always make the best choices
for my total wellbeing.
I do my best and that is enough.
I enjoy feeling supreme mobility and steady in my body.
I intend to stretch my body every day to support true freedom.
I increase overall strength to increase states of bliss.
I allow each to their own and celebrate others.
I know clearly what I am wanting in each segment of my life.
I pause and set intentions for each segment of my life.
I can easily imagine that I already have everything I desire.
My deep appreciation for life itself keeps expanding.
I can easily find things to appreciate, the list goes on and on.
I am enthusiastic for what is coming and enjoy not needing to know all the
details, I believe my creative desires will be satisfied.
As I consistently stay centred and aligned with my true-self
my responses to life will be calm and self-protecting.
I cherish and deeply appreciate the responsibility I have been given for
creating my own personal reality.
My life is an increasing experience of personal freedom.
Everything flows to increase my inner bliss.
I draw harmonious co-creators to join me in creating paradise.
Life is so much fun and so on it goes.
My appreciation eternally expands, I love greatly.
I am blessed, I am beautiful, I am flowing.
✣
Everything is spiritual,
I make my whole life a celebration.

———

SONG: 'VUELA CON EL VIENTO' (MOSE REMIX), MOSE AND AYLA SCHAFER.

A blessing for creating paradise.

I watched stars floating as the indigo sea
became luminous.
Star drops caressed my cheek.
Mesmerised by the soft, fragrant night
as my beloved blessed me,
'Do not compare yourself with anything.
Do not compare yourself with yesterday
or curse tomorrow.
Do not force a thing.
Change intentionally into your truth.
May you know you are free to who you truly are.
Your uniqueness is infinite.
Your body is pure beauty unfurling.
Your imagination illuminates the unknown.
You behold the flame of eternity within every cell.
Your listening palaces flow with wise intuition.
Upon your heart the eternal rose blooms.'

———

SONG: 'OUTER SPACE'.
ALBUM: *IN THE REAL WORLD*, ALEX SERA.

Simply let go and enjoy the art

A picture tells a thousand words,
let beauty and harmony speak deeply unto thee.
Spend time just absorbing the frequency within the artwork of
this book, nothing complicated, no over thinking,
simply allow the mystery to move through you.

✢

Art is expressing yourself freely because you realise
that there is nothing to stop you.
Art is made with star juice.
Art is eternal.
Art is innocent.
Art begins silently.
Art seeps in.
Art is unstoppable.
Art is discovered in the most unusual places.
Art is an allowing offering – take it or leave it.
Art can be seen when you close your eyes.
Art is a mirror.
Art is therapy.
Art is sensual.
Life is an art.
Art leaves a gesture for eternal contemplation.
Life is an eternal question, eternally asked by art.
Art isn't an answer, it's a beckoning portal.
Art is spirit calling you home.

✢

Practising the art of personal transformation implies
you have a powerful creative energy that you are
applying to the creation process of your life.

The Great Mystery

If you ever feel that you know everything about a subject, individual or place and there is no feeling of mystery left, HALT! You have entered the unreal reality of science, knowledge and technology with well-hidden seams and dimensions. These cold halls and spaces are filled with mirrors of distortion; there is no twinkle in the eyes of those found there, no stardust footprints or chiming whispers of the elementals, and there is no cosmic giggle either – divine chaos and mystery blocked by a cynical authority of prediction. However, depressed, compressed and limited illusionary spaces have doors which open with the light of your true divine will. If you feel lost in a cold dimension, REMEMBER to breathe deeply and declare out loud, 'I love you!' As doors swing open, run with humour and surrender into the light and magic of knowing mystery is life. To recalibrate, enter the garden of your sacred heart and sit happily on the swing of your true divine nature's good humour. Reflect upon what your body relayed to you – ask what thoughts of the not-self led you to the liminal spaces of a loveless, joyless realm?

The Great Mystery should be revered and upheld as the greatest, most sacred engine of creativity and all life ongoing, always before completion. You are one with the Great Mystery, whether you can sense this or not – and therefore, you lose the greatest part of yourself when you believe you are never going to change or there isn't any more, or you have already been there and done that. The Great Mystery is the underlying continuum in life and you should allow yourself to free ride on its magic comet tail.

This book is filled with mystery written into dreamscapes to help strengthen your imagination. Each section is based around a sense and energy centre in the subtle and physical body; you can work with this aspect to strengthen your relationship to your own creative spiritual powers. For example, Seer of Paradise enters the intuitive energy centre also known as the third eye. Rather than needing to know the science around this energy centre, playfully explore this aspect of yourself. Inspired by the dreamscapes and written prompts, cultivate a personally meaningful understanding of your intuitive and highly perceptive super powers. All your natural human, super powers are gold.

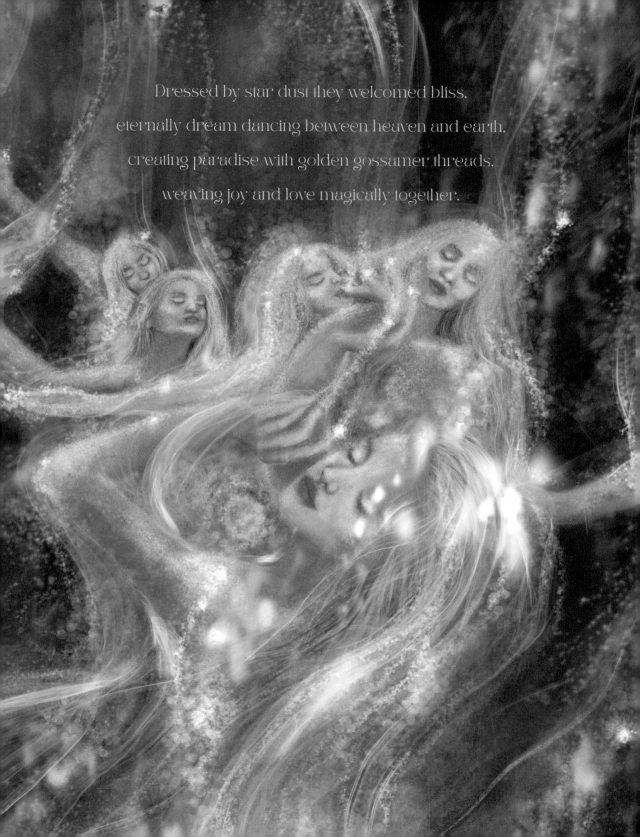

Dressed by star dust they welcomed bliss,

eternally dream dancing between heaven and earth,

creating paradise with golden gossamer threads,

weaving joy and love magically together.

I let the past and future dissolve into
the pure fragrance of joy and love - the present
moment beyond time and space - personal bliss.

Sobriety and intoxication

Through personal evolution we begin to let go of all fears as we consciously learn to intentionally adventure through time and space towards creating a life without any disharmonious entanglement.

With limited perception we may believe that being mesmerised or overwhelmed by others is a form of love and that joy may be found in a better time – equivocal to the belief that the grass is always greener on the other side of the fence. Yet true love is experienced as boundlessness and pure joy is experienced as the timelessness of simply enjoying the present moment without comparison.

To liberate yourself from limiting belief and behaviour requires less effort than you may have believed. Creative life is not about serving others first or saving anyone, it's about allowing yourself to continually learn, individuate, diversify and proactively respond to life as only the refreshingly enthusiastic true-self can. An approach that invites divine intoxication and maintains healthy emotional sobriety will facilitate personal transformation into realms of self-mastery to flow with divine bliss.

Divine intoxication is an internal mastery of appreciation for everything that is, an ability to be completely present, undisturbed by external influences, centred, grounded and relaxed while attuned to one's finer feelings and listening to a stream of super-consciousness through all the challenges of everyday life. Healthy emotional sobriety comes from understanding emotions are a guiding response to one's thoughts and beliefs. Dramatic outburst or uncontrollable sobbing is diffused by conscious awareness of one's finer feelings and releasing any negative thoughts with breathing and positive focus before the quality of one's energy becomes depleted or blocked.

You can work with this book as a way to practise being attuned to your feelings and learning to recognise what thoughts and/or beliefs are causing your body to signal disharmonious energy is manifesting your reality.

If you become overwhelmed with heightened emotions in the process of personal transformation, take a cue from the wisdom of the animal kingdom. When an animal encounters a situation which creates a fear-based response, as soon as the danger is over, they shake and twitch to release all the stress-related chemicals, returning as quickly as possible to a relaxed state of being.

Devotion

Spending quiet time in nature will always help to retune your body to a neutrality and openness to your own true divine nature – devotion to this practice leads to inner harmony. With a familiarity as to how your own true divine nature feels, you will have more sensitivity to your body's signals. If you can clearly perceive positive feelings in the body such as tingles, goosebumps and shivers of delight, you may follow those prompts to align with synchronistic opportunities and experiences. If you experience positive body signals while working with the book, write your thoughts in your journal to attune and understand yourself more deeply.

A DAILY SELF-DEVOTION PRACTICE that supports personal transformation is moving the body in ways that create mobility, flexibility and strength: clearing any stagnant, negative energy in the body, generating and storing more positive energy, liberating the radiant purity of renewal in your bone marrow, freeing potential for regeneration and growth in your bones, freeing the spine, enabling deep relaxation, dissolving any fortresses of fear surrounding cells and tempering strong desires through creating inner harmony.

If you are inspired by any habits or rituals in the dreamscapes of this book, devote to trying this behaviour for at least 40 days. Use your creative journal to document and remain devoted to the whole process.

Enter an envisioning practice to uncover a personally beneficial ritual or habit through one of the images in this book, listening to the song below as you close your eyes with the following request: 'Dear Sacred Spirit, please bring me an inspiring ritual or habit that would be beneficial and enjoyable to practise.' Breathe gently and relax, do not force anything, just observe what arises. Close the practice by thanking your spirit guides and journal any insights, inspirational guidance or realisations. You can continue working with this envisioning practice to receive healthy lifestyle practices that you are inspired to bridge into your everyday life.

SONG: 'RELAXING AMBIENT MUSIC 432HZ NATURE SOUNDS', BINAURAL BEATS, THETA WAVES MEDITATION MUSIC, RISING HIGHER MEDITATION.

YOU ARE STRONGER IN YOUR LETTING GO OF ANY CONFLICT TO FULLY ENJOY WHAT YOU LOVE AND FEELS GOOD. IMMERSE YOUR BEING IN THE LOVE STORIES THAT YOU WANT TO LIVE, TELL THEM OVER AND OVER TO YOURSELF, RELAX INTO THE PRESENT MOMENT TO MOTION THEM INTO NOW.

—

SONG: 'CCV'.
ALBUM: *WHEN WE RETURN*, SIMRIT.

Contemplation

To successfully manifest our spiritual desires, we cannot afford to give our attention to anything that will not contribute to enriching and energising our pure intent. To create lasting personal transformation, we must continue to summon and focus all our energy to that which we truly desire.

The ancient shadow of distraction stems from a doubtful fear of not being or having enough. Insatiable hunger comes from repeatedly giving one's energy to something that ultimately only depletes us.

The power of discernment, connecting with superconsciousness and an ability to say a self-appropriate 'no' is empowering and affirms: 'I am focused and happily thriving in the very generous present moment via greater infinite power. I am supported, relaxed and awake.'

The mind uses a lot of energy to properly function; if we develop a habit of slowing down the brainwave states, healthy chemistry is created that has lasting benefits and we become more open to change.

A relaxed brainwave state is a perfect and fertile environment to contemplate the sensual nature of your kind of paradise.

Throughout the book, you will find ideas towards creating your own paradisiacal experiences; contemplate the ones that most interest you and expand them through drawing, writing and collaging in your creative journal. This practice also works to refine your own personal signature.

You may like to invite friends to join you in paradisiacal contemplation and co-creation. Gather with the clear intention of dreaming about paradise together. In the gathering, enter a relaxed dream state using songs listed in this book. At the end of a designated dream time, segue into sharing all your personal visions and contemplate together how to bridge inspiring ideas into shared real life experiences. Be playful, light and non-judgemental with yourself and others present. Work on being friendly, really attentive when listening to others and open to new possibilities. Infuse the time together with laughter, dancing and enjoyment of nourishing food.

One small event at a time can grow momentum towards everlasting positive change in our communities. From little things big things grow.

SONGS: 'FOLLOW THE SUN' AND 'WE DESERVE TO DREAM'.
ALBUMS: *SPIRIT BIRD* AND *JAN JUC MOON*, XAVIER RUDD.

Genius

Experiencing your true-self's creative spirit actualised through an expression of personal genius in an invaluable human experience.

Genius is always pointed towards more life – inclusive, inspiring, illuminating and unshakeable by doubters or overthinking. Genius cannot be explained away, it is unashamedly omnipresent. Genius glows in the dark.

Try the following practice to uncover your own genius.

Imagine softly placing a bejewelled veil of self-appreciation over your whole being. Sit quietly to feel your depth with luminous clarity; see if you can exist at least for a moment without any judgement. Focus upon breathing with a warm, soft smile as you imagine a rose upon your heart bloom, then open any page of this book and absorb the words and image. Let your feelings flow in a stream, become the observer, place yourself high on a soft cloud to lovingly witness yourself. Open your creative journal to a new page and begin to write. It doesn't matter what you write, just keep writing until your words become flames of convergence, enlightening aspects of yourself ready to be expressed and seen. This practice of communion with your superconsciousness should be a playful and lightly enthusiastic process of enquiry – listening and attuning to the subtle responses in your body. This practice cultivates greater self-trust and awareness of the genius living within you awaiting permission to playfully emerge and be polished with the light of your self-acceptance and genuine appreciation.

Look into your personal birth mandala*, Gene Keys* and or Human Design*, and study what genius resides in your cosmic potential. Can you alchemise your totality into a contemporary expression of your divinity? Do you know what kind of creativity your genius points you towards?

Being enjoyably honest with oneself blesses the creating of paradise with honesty as foundation – from little things big things grow.

By nature you touch life with your intentional focus; could you allow your genius out of the bottle to permeate your life like a mist of love so powerful that you begin to dissolve mountains that you once thought impassable?

SONG: 'FREEDOM', MOSE AND MATIA KALLI.

*See Resources, page 262.

Life lived as a creative celebration

perpetuates freedom.

My life is real joy

and real love woven together

with the magic of an appreciative,

liberated heart.

As I sit here now I can sense something stirring
within me never before so clearly felt.
I am sensing a connection that moistens my eyes.
We are always amongst dear, wise and benevolent elders.
The rocks, the mountains, the sky, the sea,
the flowers and grasses are each and all elders to me.
Gaia is the wise one - the divine immortal elder.

Humour

Have you ever sat silently in the beauty of nature and listened for the COSMIC GIGGLE? Have you witnessed a crystalline dragonfly effortlessly moving in all directions, felt velvet butterfly wings brushing your skin, been swept up in the rhythmic intelligence of trees bowing in the breeze, imagined elementals dancing on your head? Is innocent wonderment paradise found?

As you work through this book, practise not taking anything too seriously. Become more observant as you entertain whimsy; make a commitment to go to places of natural beauty; cultivate a connection to the sky, bodies of water, mountains, rocks, trees, birds, insects and animals. Listen to moving water, the wind, birdsong and other natural sounds while imagining that each sound holds a personal message – contemplate lightly what that might be. Imagine the elementals are mischievously leaving you messages; keep a look out for anything that speaks to your heart and activates a sense of your own innocence. A visceral knowing of the elementals will come if you spend enough time with mountains, oceans, rivers, trees, flowers, plants, rocks, insects, fungi, animals, birds, sea life and sky.

Self-enquiry: how can I fully express my appreciation so my influence upon this highly impressionable field of infinite possibilities returns to activate creative perception and lightness of being in myself?

Each of our senses are naturally activated through being captivated by nature's harmonic codes of creative consciousness. Connecting with higher levels of consciousness through sensual enjoyment of the natural world is a healing salve. Connecting to the purity of nature with appreciation and wonder leads to fresh perspectives. As nature beckons us to be held by the magnificence and magic of the present moment, our deepest sense of the lightness of our true-self comes to the surface.

✦

Pouring your heart into life aligned with the abundance of nature is the beginning of receiving the true gold of thriving. Write love letters, songs and poems from your creative journal onto beautiful paper; go into nature and leave them as an offering and blessing for Gaia and her nature spirits.

SONG: 'MANY MOONS' (REMIX), MOSE, BACHAN KAUR AND BINDER.

Imagination and illumination

Many dreamscapes in this book are visions of the principle of synarchy – harmonious joint rulership with a view that no individual is more important than another – an evolutionary approach to co-creation.

The underlying creative power and great dreamer central to this book is beloved Gaia. As you read contemplate how much she supports humanity, allow any fears of lack and wounds of abandonment to be healed.

Another signature of this work is the distinction between time and place is sometimes dissolved. If you allow yourself to enter the book's dreamscapes with a curious mind, perception of your own multi-dimensionality may increase. Through imagining that you are boundless and timeless – existing beyond one perception – you may illuminate a deeper sense of your totality.

This book leads you to connect with your own superconsciousness – a very broad perspective focused towards inner harmony and a compassionate guide towards taking very good care of your mind and body, being light-hearted, present to enjoy and align with the beauty and harmony of the natural world and creative cosmos.

As you read become the custodian of magic wormholes – portals of your imagination that you may enter to discover new ways of being that transcend what has manifested, illuminating genuine freshness leading to unified beauty.

Life is an ENERGY DANCE: learn how to balance yourself between heaven and earth; be grounded with love and joy as you ascend like the ROSE DRAGON.

I love who I am, I love what I create, I love how I move.
I love how when I cultivate silence, smile and relax,
good things emerge from deep within me.
I love pausing to enjoy the beauty within and all surrounding.
I appreciate every smell, taste, sight, touch and sound is
offering inspiring clarity for luminous self-expression.
I am present, relaxed and open to guidance from
harmonious, benevolent, broader perspectives.
I deeply appreciate and listen to my true-self.
I draw beauty, harmony, joy and love into my experiences.
My appreciation for my life continues to expand.

SONGS: 'THE DANCE AND THE WONDER' (MOSE REMIX), MOSE AND SAM GARRETT. 'OFFERING', MOSE, ALEXANDRE LORA AND MATIA KALLI.

YOU ARE THE ROSE,
THE LOVER AND
THE STAR OF ALL
YOUR DREAMS.

Letting go

As you work through this book, you may enjoy also working with my *Let Go* mini reading card deck – created many moons ago.

Cultivating practices that support a truly enjoyable and ultimately blissful personal transformational journey is essential if you are to wake up in a paradise of your own creation.

Supporting practices include bathing in sunlight, floating in water, immersing in sound and dance, being held in a beloved's arms, enjoying the fragrance of flowers, being in the energy of a forest, bathing in moonlight, writing poetry, being in good company, raves of self-appreciation, praise of all that is and inviting openness to change.

If you have the good fortune to be able to visit a natural hot spring or drink natural spring water on a regular basis embrace this opportunity and fully receive the blessing that it is.

If you are inspired to travel to certain places or absorb different and diverse cultures, can you work towards living those dreams?

If you are inspired to become creative in new and unusual ways do not hesitate to let inspiration take you into joyful abandon of all self-repression. Do not be afraid of anything – least of all your innocent desires and genuinely unique creative impulses. Get lost every evening in the golden light of your own glorious starlight and enjoy intimately floating within the greatness of your mysterious true-self.

May you become the enlightened gardener of your great dreams.
May the elementals dance in your heart's garden,
bringing freshness and wildness.
May the wellspring of your eternal self flow freely.
May you let go of perspectives that hold you back.
May you experience the unconditional, unified luminous field.

ALBUM: *LOVE IS SPACE*, DEVA PREMAL.

STAY OPEN TO FRESHNESS
AND ENTER THE GLITTERING FIELD
OF EVOLUTIONARY POSSIBILITY.

Remembering
ONENESS

Immerse yourself in an intimate sense of oneness
with the creative source - embrace your innocence.

÷

Togetherness comes from a sense of oneness.
Bliss comes from a sense of oneness to true-self.
Fluid evolution into true-self comes from the undivided self.
A sense of oneness alleviates aversion to humanity.
A sense of oneness affords genuine warmth and compassion.
A sense of oneness inspires appreciation for everything.
A sense of oneness opens a very broad perspective.
A sense of oneness invites fresh wonderment.
A sense of oneness brings transforming realisations.
A sense of oneness creates twinkling eyes and a warm smile.

÷

Don't be distracted by anything untoward, let it go. Surrender your attention to personal bliss.
You can breathe underwater, you can swim all by yourself.
The air is full of water, you are swimming through life.
There is no need to hold onto anything.

÷

Each must release themselves from their own suffering.
Breathe, be simply nourished, all will be well.
Let go of any judgements and listen to your singing heart.
Relax, you have nothing to prove.
Be your own beloved and true lovers will come.
You are magnetic, attract with appreciative focus.
You are powerful, evolve with great love.
Guide your focus towards your joyful eternal nature.

÷

There is nothing outside of you that can make you feel whole,
you are already whole, complete before completion.

÷

The paradox of our life's love story is that we believe we want
a happy ending but we have no ultimate end.
As we are the eternal journey, it is wise to focus on the quality of the journey, not the destination.
You are complete and eternal, forever unfurling unto thee.
It's time to float through the sacred air, to fly, to cruise – deeper
into love, joy and the bliss of being in the now.
You are free to keep learning and experiencing life.
Wisdom, strength and contentment come through softness.
Give yourself permission to enjoy yourself here now.
A sense of oneness is bliss.

Plenty

The sweetness of life beckons a deeper connection and rekindling of one's truly adventurous spirit, upholding a joy of the journey without needing to know all the details. A true sense of oneness energetically aligns us to the plentiful field of possibility and miraculous synchronicities.

Life is a game of choice, but beware what may enter your psyche if you entertain the idea that this reality is some kind of hunger game. Life is meant to be fun and delightfully playful.

From where you are now you may enter a true and certain paradise by aligning with the seasons of Gaia – within the energy of each season is a wonder-filled continuum of plenty, variety and nourishment for the unfolding of personal transformation. The harmonious changes present within each season bring the stability that only continuous and fluid change can offer.

This shared reality is expanding with everyone's desires; it's a wonderland of plenty for those who have no aversion to receiving. There is no experience of lack to be had for those who can effortlessly breathe and smile as they cherish and deeply appreciate being alive. Right now is a wonderful place to begin refreshingly new adventures – trust there will always be plenty to nourish you along the way.

The fruits of pure enjoyment are everywhere and for everyone who believes they exist. The fruits of appreciation are easily grown by an intentional thinker and are deliciously satisfying for everyone. The fruits of delightful potential and the juiciness of ideas ripe for creating are in everyone you meet. The fruits of liberty hang within easy reach on every branch of life, in every colourful expression of being human. The fruit of sweetness flows from every open heart and authentic warm smile. The infinite fruits of paradise grow freely in all flavours from free-spirited, consciously creative thinkers.

You are free to be very satisfied with your innocent and wild humanness and should be very excited for what is next. In your creative journal draw a vibrant, strong and eternal tree of life and decorate it with the fruits of genuine warmth, high regards, praise and appreciation for Gaia, her seasons and all the treasures life has granted you.

SONG: 'NATIVE PRAYER', GERHARD FANKHAUSER AND EINAT GILBOA.

Innocence

You can never fully know what is coming to you next as you are innocent in each moment of your life. As each individual continually reprioritises and changes that which is most wanted, the co-experienced reality must reorganise to deliver what is being called forth.

Rather than thinking of your experiences as karmic, consider that they are simply what everyone has been asking for by focus of their attention – either deliberately or not. Life is a shared dream with infinite storytellers.

As you master deliberate creative focus without being negatively distracted, align your subconscious mind's habitual functions to support your conscious beliefs, and commune with your superconsciousness, you will experience oneness between your different levels of consciousness.

If something is pulling you away from your naturally good-feeling true-self, it's not worth your attention. The sooner you can drop any thinking about anything that doesn't feel good and dissolve any defensiveness around your innocent impulses to be included in life, the better the outcome.

As you uphold feeling deeply satisfied for the magnificent potential of life itself and a deeply appreciative outlook – even if that requires some dedicated practice – you will be delighted and surprised as the things you are wanting materialise in the most wonderful ways.

When you embody the timeless patience of joy and the boundless adventure of love in a whole state of being – yin and yang unified – you will experience increasing states of oneness. Creating paradise happens in the unified field. Contemplate and journal what aspects of your life can be brought together and unified through appreciation and compassion.

SONG: 'SONG OF THE STARS'.
ALBUM: *SEVATI*, MIRABAI CEIBA.

DON'T EVER TURN
YOURSELF UPSIDE
DOWN TO PLEASE
ANYONE ELSE.

Unify

Everything has a natural rhythm and with your calm, unified focus of attention you can witness energy sequentially and serendipitously motioning towards creation of precisely what is being asked for.

The pressure of performance in daily life need not become self-harmful stress. A practice of conscious discernment which guides focus towards what is actually important in each moment and what is clearly the next right action stems from a relaxed and neutral mind.

A daily practice of meditation with intentional, slow, deep breathing will facilitate centring and unification of self. Extremely positive and negative perspectives are subdued with a superconscious perspective creating a healthy neutral mind. In deeper meditative states, consciously focused upon directing the breath and infusing the breath with gratitude and positive future blessings can work to heal and enlighten.

The rhythm of a unified heart and mind intelligence, relaxed and present to sequentially process life, informs the body that everything needed is readily available in the present moment. By allowing the heart intelligence to sing the ocean of the mind into calm waves, the body rejoices and the irrigation network of the fascia through the body can perform the magic of bringing nourishment to every cell. Everything improves when you practise existing in a unified state of being – allowing a natural flow of energy, cultivating happiness just for being alive and feeling a part of the whole.

For liberty
I behold you in the power of your unity.
I behold you in the power of your beauty.
I behold you in the power of your harmony.
I behold you in the grace of being fully alive.
The true-self is who you are.
You are supported, blessed and appreciated.
Om shanti, om shanti, om shanti.
Peace, peace, peace.

SONG: 'CURA CORAZÓN', MOSE.

The surrender

Delicious.
Simply delicious.
Savoured.
Enjoyed very slowly.
No haste.
No force.
Sweet relief.
Sweet release.
She was done with suffering.
She had become calmly disinterested in
giving attention to those that complained.
Calmly and quietly.
Clean and easy.
She dropped all habits of being distracted.
She happily surrendered to creating paradise.
She became pure creation in motion.
Her life was seamlessly woven together with
gossamer dreams and fire-stars.
ANOTHER DREAMER AWAKENS WITHIN THE DREAM.

GAIA'S DREAM

As an eternal, sacred being,
I welcome good things coming.
I send my blessings into the infinite field.
I dream that all creatures of my world
are free to make love and joy real -
leading to natural states of bliss.
And the golden spirit of bliss
leads us all to creating paradise.
We are eternal - and so it is.
As you enter these dreamscapes, can you perceive the
golden spirit of bliss creatively weaving beauty, unity,
harmony and peace through Gaia's forever new dreams?

SONG: 'GAYATRI MANTRA'.
ALBUM: *GALIM*, LEMON AND SOUL & OR MAHAPATRA.

Dream of the golden one

When our sun – of infinite suns – birthed our universe, great intention was seeded with blessings for freedom of thought and expression, calling upon evolutionary forces to eternally weave new fractal patterns.

As Gaia formed she began to evolve by thinking completely unique and beautiful ideas. Branches of the great book – The Tree of Life – began to grow stronger, preparing to record all of the planet's new and real experiences.

As life evolved on her watery body, new dreamscapes were very, very slowly bridged into reality, and she realised incredible patience would be required to arrive at the harmony, beauty, unity and peace that her heart truly wanted.

Through Gaia's virtue she discovered how to turn lead into gold, leading to evolutionary leaps in all her dreams. As she held faith, kept dreaming and believing, her dreams became bigger, capturing the minds and hearts of stars throughout the universe. As no one was excluded in Gaia's dreams, many were attracted to her unique ideas of unity and beauty.

After many eons of establishing virtues upon her planet, Gaia created a golden light thread – incredibly fine, strong and beyond normal perception. Tiny etheric spiders from the heart of Gaia's most beautiful and paradisiacal places came forth to be cosmic messengers. Gaia gave the etheric spiders the codes needed to make the golden light thread and these master weavers set to work upon the noble task. They first anchored the golden light thread in great trees and then lifted themselves into the cosmos with spirals of golden light thread trailing behind them. The spiders travelled far and wide, entering the dreams of dreamers who held seeds of good intentions compatible to Gaia's great dream of physical immortality, leaving them with a golden thread of connection to Gaia.

Stars with virtuous seeds continue to be invited and welcomed to Gaia to become the new ones – water bearers working with golden light in creative ways to initiate the Golden Age. The great diversity and uniqueness of these dreamers ensures life ongoing; the great changes that they bring create incredible stability and brilliance. As the new ones emerge many others are activated to REMEMBER why they are here at this time.

SONG: 'AS YOU WILL' [SHYE BEN TZUR COVER], NESSI GOMES.

The seeds of Ananda, dreaming together

*Evolution leads to a natural state of bliss.
Through exotic, wild, unique and
intoxicatingly beautiful expressions of life,
we eternally realise who we are in truth.*

Venus was dreaming of a divinely beautiful and unique planet when a voice of immense light penetrated her visions as Jupiter spoke with cosmic luminosity and beneficent command: 'It is time for independence my beloved daughter.'

When Venus and her two sisters left the orbit of Jupiter, their journey was both exhilarating and chaotic. Due to hesitation and the incredible magnetism of Jupiter, it took many eons before they found a clear and independent path to explore the cosmos. They ultimately found the precious jewel they were searching for – a new planet of all shades of blues and greens. Mists of love swirled across her curves of splendid magnificence. Joyous songs came from her sparkling oceans and her expansive skies hummed with new life. Venus and her sisters were intrigued and in love with her completely.

'She is the real paradise of our creation dream!' exclaimed Venus to her beloved sisters. Feeling deeply inspired they entered Gaia's dreams and spoke with her, sharing their visions of the beauty, joy, harmony and unity that they could create together.

Venus concluded: 'Grace shall be born from our creations and even though war may be declared many times over the roses we bring, the divine rose of life, love, creativity and fragrant beauty will bloom upon the cross of her matter forever – always before completion.'

Gaia stirred, breathing deeply in agreement as rainbows and mists of love appeared in all directions across the aspects of her body bathing in sunlight.

The sisters breathed deeply together and in ecstatic celebration released an ambrosial nectar from their cosmic bodies. Those who witnessed this event of heavenly purity, were initiated as carriers of golden light expressing as exquisite creativity and embodied beauty through many earth-bound lifetimes in preparation to emerge as awakened sacred humans heralding the golden age of Aquarius.

SONG: 'NATURALEZA'.
ALBUM: *ALIENTO*, DANIT.

Retelling a creation story

When Venus and her sisters first approached Gaia they found her energy field to be incredibly magnetic. To ensure they didn't collide due to the immensity of their sheer physical attraction, they formed a divine trinity, and so as one bright star they came closer to Gaia.

Their first meeting created immense fireworks as they creatively related with joyous enthusiasm and appreciation. Gaia was very agreeable to their ideas for co-creativity. They left her field to further contemplate, stabilise and refine their dreams, promising to return.

The majority of humans who experienced those early encounters were very confused and fearful of the powerful fire-star that had suddenly appeared, showering their land with fire seeds, then mysteriously disappearing for hundreds of years.

As Venus and her sisters refined their relationship with Gaia, they also refined their orbit around her highly charged energy field, ultimately creating a stable and beautiful flower pattern. For many eons their divine relationship was generally misunderstood by any humans who feared the unknown and the fire of creative power. Catastrophic myths of separation, sacrifice and death were repeatedly told, warning of the existence of uncontrollable and mysterious feminine cosmic powers, seeding a fear of the unknown and the divine feminine deep into the psyche of humanity.

As we evolve and our evolutionary perspective refines, higher truth always segues into an ability to embody grace. As our earthly love story is never-ending, fresh perspectives are born every moment which lead to beauty and unifying evolutionary occurrences.

The real beginning of this love story was born of a desire for divine beauty to be realised – a continuum of earthly individuals sweetly and courageously dreaming with beautiful intentions to live in harmony and peace have declared this will be forever so.

·:·

Imagine your own starseed journey; write any inspired musings in your journal.

———

SONG: 'AMAZING GRACE' (FEAT. PAUL KELLY).
ALBUM: *THE GOSPEL ALBUM*, GURRUMUL.

It's time for new life-affirming,
creative dream stories.

Timeless and boundless creation codes
are foundational to life
held within every individual's cells
activated through conscious intention
to create beauty, peace, harmony and unity.

You are here to liberate and celebrate
your unlimited creative potential.

A PROMISE MADE AND KEPT IS
A MOST POWERFUL GESTURE.
A VERY CLEAR CREATIVE
INTENTION THAT IS
BLESSED BY LIBERTY AND
CELEBRATION IS FREED
BEYOND TIME AND SPACE.
BEAUTY IS LIFE BLOOMING
UNSTOPPABLE AND ETERNAL.

—

ALBUM: *ALEINTO*, DANIT.

Imagine and contemplate each flower is a portal to grace

Imagine that flowers are precious gifts from the inspiring fire seeds of the Venusians and every flower a portal to beauty and grace beyond the mortal coil and what has been.

The gardens of heaven on earth that grow from the seeds of love and joy continue to dissolve separation stories and inspire highly beneficial and harmonious relationships. Flowers bring people together in ways that were not imagined possible before thousands of different fragrant flowers bloomed across the planet. Flowers offer a timeless and boundless language beyond the analytical thinking mind and a shy lover's apprehension.

Can you imagine what it was like to witness the first flowers blooming in the soil made fertile by the Venusian fires? Contemplate the nature of a blessing that is not first comprehended and what is required to see its true blessings.

Contemplate the eternal amazing grace given to humans through the divine inspiration to grow gardens filled with beauty and share what is grown, in right relationship with the land, all creatures and plants.

Contemplate the power of the soft, gentle, colourful, quiet, still and fragrant beauty of flowers to endlessly inspire creative expressions of appreciation, romantic love and friendship.

Spend time looking into a flower, then close your eyes with the intention of entering its portal into divine creation. In your creative journal write, paint or draw from any inspired visions or insights that come through the dreaming.

The divine creative power of beauty is to transform absolutely everything – beauty comes from eternal life, eternal life comes from beauty. Have you ever begun to create something that you intended to be beautiful but given up before you finished either because you or others had judged it unworthy? Working with your flower dream visions, decide to create something beautiful; remain devoted to see the process through from raw beauty into an offering of golden light that shines through the mundane.

Creating a subtle experience of intoxication

The divine experience of bliss is an embodiment of eternal creative light. When an individual merges heaven and earth within, embodying their inner joy and love through living well, liberated from the influence of the over-culture, their life becomes an infinitely expanding, blissful experience.

At first encounter the subtle realms of experience are beyond any words, silent in essence, yet overflowing with information. Consider the subtle nature of a flower's fragrance, this defined signature of energy permeates the space around it with a distinctive note, a divine song vibrating above our ear's normal hearing range. Flowers are communicating through a unified field, their fragrance extending an invitation into our physical dimension from their unknown realms of existence, beckoning us to enter unity consciousness. When we are relaxed and present wandering through a fragrant garden, we can enter that unified field, reminded of our true divine nature and our interconnected relationship with all that is.

Practise holding noninvasive, incorruptible creative presence throughout your day. Work upon moving gracefully through the world, with great self-awareness, mastering fluid movement and discretion. If you encounter any disharmonious situations, rather than defend yourself, you can try deepening and slowing your breath to uphold a naturally blissful state that has flower-like qualities. You may imagine inner personal bliss creating alchemical magic, so instead of producing fear pheromones, your body is releasing a highly subtle signature fragrance like an exquisite flower. You may imagine you also have thorns like a rose so you are naturally protected. As you begin to enter the world of flowers you'll discover you are also an alchemical magician, able to effortlessly activate resonant aspects of higher consciousness in others. You may hone the capability of charmingly disarming whoever you encounter, activating a unified acknowledgement of your shared humanity and all the blessings of your meeting. Imagine releasing a lasting, inspirational impression wherever you go as you masterfully work with the subtle fields of energy. Imagine that as you shine a light of appreciation towards what is beautiful and harmonious, it helps others notice and appreciate beauty and harmony too.

SONG: 'FLUYENDO'.
ALBUM: *SILENT VOICES*, AYLA SCHAFER.

Kiss
flowers

Blooming just happens when you allow

Imagine a rising archetype – humans who have mastered continuously blissful aliveness. I name this group the Anandians: the word 'ananda' comes from the ancient language of Sanskrit, translated in simple terms as bliss. Continue to imagine as I describe this archetype.

Anandians evolve naturally and harmoniously within the society to which they are born. With mature, unified awareness they decide to disengage from all unnecessary stress and drama completely, happily maintaining a calm yet ever-changing relationship with life itself.

Anandians are typically drawn to nature and cherish quietly observing the beauty of all life. They resonate greatly with the joy and beauty of flowers, entering a deeply appreciative, dreamy state infused with potent visions of the highest potential of their own self-expression. This self-awareness inspires them to go beyond social norms and explore their full, uniquely creative potential. They intuitively understand there is no reason to explain themselves or their choices to any other, choosing to discreetly explore being fully alive without any self-repression or doubt.

Anandians are extremely good listeners, especially to their inner knowing. They experience personal enrichment as they take good care of their mind and body with joyous thoughts, vibrant food, fluid movement, meditative and contemplative states, and natural self-expression as they co-create and relate with others. They reach a point where they simply can't take life too seriously; everything becomes a muse to their creativity and bliss finds them everywhere and they find it in everything.

Anandians can self-actualise as an embodiment of bliss at any age and are each highly unique. They do not follow any strict regimes of behaviour or ritual, preferring to playfully refine their lifestyle and routines to suit the whimsical nature of ever-changing personal desires. These divine humans are masters of the spiritualisation of matter.

✢

If this inspires you in anyway use your creative journal to expand upon this concept. Can you imagine yourself belonging to this archetype?

SONG: 'MORI SHEJ'.
ALBUM: *FOUR GREAT WINDS*, PEIA.

I surrender the

beginning & end.

Weaving the
BELONGING
Story

Living in an abundant flow

When instructing the young how to socially behave, the underlying expectation and tone of delivery is crucial to their perception. For example, if a child is required to be grateful when they are only given what they need when they display a particular behaviour, a belief that receiving abundance is highly conditional can be instilled. With this in consideration, a gratitude practice may resonate with the conscious mind of that individual as an adult but an underlying subconscious belief may block receptivity to abundance based on perception of conditions.

We cannot block our desire for more, it is a natural human inclination born out of every single thing we experience no matter how satisfied we are. As humans we are designed to seek expansion through our interactions with contrast of all kinds to orientate us towards evolutionary refinement.

Appreciation, praise and gratitude have similar but different frequencies; each can be utilised to raise your thoughts to a frequency that matches natural abundance. It is highly beneficial to appreciate another's good fortune as you are in agreement with good things flowing to everyone, yourself included. Being filled with gratitude and overflowing with contentment matches the frequency of the abundance of life. Praise has a frequency akin to sprinkling gold dust upon everything, whatever you praise is lifted with the frequency of divine blessings.

Say the following affirmations out loud and sit quietly attuning to your emotional response to each. You may like to shake your hands and/or body before and in-between each to clear your energy. There is no right or wrong response – this exercise is designed to help you to perceive which perspective has the least energetic resistance from your body. Once you have a clear perception, you can work with the most powerful option to cultivate a deeper sense of belonging and healthy relationship with living in abundance.

I radiate with gratitude for my beautiful and abundant life.

I radiate with appreciation for my beautiful and abundant life.

I radiate with praise for my beautiful and abundant life.

SONG: 'MAMA', SAM GARRETT AND MOLLIE MENDOZA.

You belong to life.

Connected to the golden creative thread
the gossamer song of life.

Allow the joy and love that exists within
your centre to expand softly.

Seeing with the eyes of the beloved place yourself
at the centre of your own existence.

Wrap yourself in your own love
and joy with enthusiasm.

Embody a love of life.

Forever becoming

*Your dharma is not a linear biology, you are destined
to dive through portals and take quantum leaps through
clear and certain conscious awareness of your experience.
You are always so much more than you can perceive
and more expansive than you can ever remember.
Relax into the joyous quietude of your heart –
enjoy feeling into the silent knowing –
you belong to life on earth,
forever alive in the heart of Gaia.
Listen to the belonging songs of the whales and didgeridoo.
You are free to embody adventure through your pure heart,
you belong to both adventure and a beautiful home.
You are awakening to the totality of you,
don't turn away from being more,
you will find joyousness and
exquisite harmony of your true-self
forever in your heart and in the heart of Gaia.
Your dharma is the exquisiteness of your own rhythm,
harmoniously co-creating what has never been.
You made a wild, cosmic promise to awaken no matter what,
and upon becoming Seer, continue forward,
rejoicing your aliveness with a full commitment to courageously
receive what you are wanting and to offer your gifts freely.
In agreement to creating paradise, you open to receive yourself,
the true beloved – all self-repression
and self-denial dissolve into nothing.
This love story is always before completion,
always working out better than you can imagine.
Om shanti, om shanti, om shanti.
Peace, peace, peace.*

SONG: 'JAI SHIVA SHANKAR', FRANKO HEKE, MONICA DOGRA AND MOSE.

An ancient future dream

As you enter these dreamscapes can you feel a sense of deep belonging to earth? Do you feel the gold of evolutionary potential instilled deep within every cell of your body?

✦

She swam to the surface of the emerald sea, propped herself upon a rocky outcrop and gazed up into the inky night sky where orbs and star streams danced around the whales and dolphins. The music of the spheres resounding with whale song and the cosmic 'om'. He swam up to join her, their warm, wet bodies lightly touching and tingling upon connection.

'There are places you haven't been where you belong, I sense you understand this call deeply,' he spoke quietly as he gazed into her light green eyes. She smiled with deep appreciation and understanding, knowing this part of the journey was not for him, kissing him lightly on the lips.

'I am responding to Gaia's great dream, it may come to you one day too; it's about making joy and love real through an eternal creation of paradise. I believe in this dream – it feels as it is already so.' She smiled warmly at him again and blew him a kiss: 'Until we meet again my dear beloved friend.'

She closed her eyes as blue-green colours rose from the top of her head and swirled through her auric field forming a smooth and luminous orb around her whole being. She floated up into the sky joining the procession of divine beings as they were carried by a strong astral current in the cosmic plasma ocean through wormholes that led to a deep ocean portal of Gaia.

She swam through the blue ocean with the whales and dolphins, recalibrating to the new atmosphere. They entered warm waters where she rested in a deeply meditative state, patiently waiting. As she floated, she was shown visions of a lush green landscape, a clear vision of an entrance to a cave behind a waterfall left a lasting impression.

She floated gently in timelessness until she heard a woman singing her name: 'Mei, Mei, Mei.' Sea flowers opened in response, releasing a fluorescent nectar that shot to the surface.

Mei swam up towards the growing light and dissolved into its intensity. After her surrendering she became aware of floating in an incredible space of warmth and softness.

SONG: 'DEELAHLI'.
ALBUM: *OSTRICONI*, YEAHMAN & MINA SHANKHA

Water birth dreaming

In the long ago dreaming, a magnificent island rose out of the calm, pacific ocean. Gaia dreamed the island to be inhabited with an abundant and divine variety of life without any predatory animal species. Through her dreams she inspired humans to travel across the ocean to the island and ensured that they were settled and safe. As they began to flourish Gaia invited the Star Mothers in another dream, inspiring them to bring their seeds of golden light to create a sacred human that would one day embody all virtues of true divinity. The Star Mothers came, integrating their inner light and spiritual customs into lives of humans in the watery world. They coupled with the male islanders to birth humans of great beauty and warmth seeded with the light of the one soul – the unstoppable spiritualisation of matter had begun.

Many moons and lifetimes after the Star Mothers first came, Gaia sent out another dream, calling starseeds ready to be born with the desire to create completely new ways of being human towards becoming immortal with her.

÷

The Star Mother Melei knew it was time to give birth to her daughter, she called her sisters with Mei's sweet song. Singing together they walked arm in arm to the birthing pools. The sisters helped Melei into the warm salty water of a crystal clear rock pool by the gentle, tropical ocean. They scattered frangipani, ylang ylang, jasmine and hibiscus flowers onto the water, rubbed coconut oil onto Melei's tanned, naked body and put more flowers in her hair as they swept it up to the crown of her head.

Birthing was guided by mother and child, synchronised with slow and rhythmic breathing, calmly riding waves of intensity into the full surrender that followed. Sisters worked with Melei and her unborn child for hours, taking turns to offer support and joyous nurture. The sisters lit candles as the sky softened to a dusky pink and they poured sweetly scented oils through the water. Just as the full moon began to rise, Melei let out a joyful cry and pulled her baby up onto her heart.

The sisters gathered as Melei laughed and cried, 'This is Mei, sweet Mei!'

Upon hearing her name Mei opened her lungs and deeply inhaled the evening's sweet air – the smell of earth made an unforgettable impression.

Star child
dreaming

Mei always squealed with delight when she was taken to the river or the ocean, wanting to stay in the water for hours. When she could talk, she told everyone she was a fish person, her family would laugh at her innocence, and even though she firmly declared it to be true, they would never believe her.

When Mei saw dolphins she said: 'They are my family too!' Her family humoured her, nodding and winking to one another. Mei noticed this and felt all kinds of energy swirling through her body – she became hot in the face and looked the other way as little tears fell upon her cheeks. Something caught Mei's attention and, looking into the crystalline sea, she heard a soothing voice.

MOTHER WATER spoke and sung directly to her: 'You are made from heaven and earth, you know who you are in truth, relax and trust, you are so very beautiful, made for great adventure and creation. Flow like water, bend like the palm trees, stay soft like clouds and strong as rolling thunder. Only do what feels good to you – you belong where there is only love and joy.'

At night Mei often lay awake wondering who she was and where she came from.

As she listened to the ocean, looking out her window at the stars, she felt certain shooting stars fell deep into the ocean.

Mei also loved spending hours in the village gardens, exploring wild nature; she truly loved the smell of the earth. Frangipanis were her favourite flowers and she would adorn herself with as many as possible, stringing more onto leis to wear and give to her mother and aunties.

The Star Mothers were very strong and clear in their guidance for village life. To ensure the survival of their people they expected their guidelines to be followed. Young Mei tried to adhere to the customs and traditions of her tribe but she was deeply influenced by MOTHER WATER'S ongoing encouragement to remain free and unique. Mei adventured on through life, inquisitively playful and experimenting newly.

✦

Prepare to go into a dream while listening to the ocean soundtrack and working with the previous dream sequence stories and/or the images. Be open and receptive. When you are finished your dreaming session, journal anything inspiring or insightful.

SONG: 'MEDITATION OCEAN', ANUGAMA.

Dreaming of liberty

Prompted to look to the ocean, Mei saw a pod of dolphins playing close to the shore. She ran into the water and swam out to join them. Once she came close to the dolphins, they quietly swam in a circle around her. Mei laid back, closing her eyes, floating in the blissful energy, her heart ecstatic with an overwhelming flush of peaceful pleasure. Her changing body felt attractive; she enjoyed the feeling of her breasts and soft, new curves as she moved through the water. When she opened her eyes, the dolphins were gone and she noticed a tiny sea dragon floating beside her.

'Look at you, so beautiful!' exclaimed Mei.

It looked at her with its bright green eyes and spoke directly into her heart: 'You are here to experience great adventure, but first you must become deeply grounded in communion with your inner voice. Be guided by what feels good and follow the natural laws. Allow yourself to be quiet and retreat when you are guided – you will be a witness to great evolution. Don't force yourself to do anything you don't want to, be guided by the intelligence of your inner essence; there is always a harmonious way through any challenge. Gaia supports you to prosper, together you are dreaming eternal paradise to be real.' The tiny sea dragon then disappeared into the watery light of a rising crystalline wave.

Mei lay back and floated in the warm water, enjoying a sense of belonging to the great, sacred mystery of life. She fearlessly dove under a wave, promising to honour what felt good to her.

✦

Contemplate the time in your life when your body was first deeply transforming through adolescence; notice what feelings arise as you bring this time to mind. Self-enquire if you have any feelings of aversion or shame. Now contemplate how you feel about undergoing personal transformation: are there any correlating feelings or does it feel completely different to you? Your answers will give you insights as to where healing work may be done to liberate you from any fears related to experiencing deep and complete personal change.

SONG: 'THE WATER BLESSING SONG' (MOSE & BINDER REMIX), MOSE AND NALINI BLOSSOM.

'IT'S OKAY TO ALLOW
YOURSELF TO BE FREE,
TO CHOOSE HOW TO
THINK FOR YOURSELF,'
WHISPERED THE TREES.

Dreaming
a la naturale

On the way back to the village, Mei heard the conch announcing the cousins' whaling boats upon the horizon. She found Maleko in the palm grove, sitting in the shade eating coconuts. They had infrequently played together as children, only recently discovering a deeper attraction.

Maleko stopped eating, looked directly at Mei and said: 'I love your ocean eyes.' He drew closer, kissing her ever so softly and then paused waiting for her to respond. She kissed him back on the lips and they fell to the lush grass while embracing and caressing one another.

Gathering their things they ran laughing together into the beach jungle. Without hesitation they explored intimacy together guided by what felt the most incredibly enjoyable.

As Mei slid through the gardens back to her hut the trading celebrations had begun. She heard one of the cousins speaking to an elder: 'I would like to take the ocean-eye girl with me.'

Mei gasped and then paused to centre herself, she felt empowered as she imagined quietly leaving the village. She went to her hut, gathered some essential supplies and left.

After she climbed the first mountain Mei paused to contemplate, and she was guided to a secluded valley. When she entered the tranquil haven, rushing water drew her attention to a beautiful waterfall. A small path led her to a hidden cave behind the waterfall just as her dreaming vision had shown and upon entering she found a perfect place to stay.

As she sat looking out of the cave, a sparkling energy in the waterfall spoke into her heart: 'Welcome Mei, what a blessing you have trusted your sense of belonging to the creative adventure of life.'

✢

If you feel inspired create a personal dreaming story from this dream sequence. If it were your dream how would creatively express or describe it. What would be the next sequence/s?

**SONG: 'TRYAMBAKAM' (FEAT. CHANDRA LACOMBE).
ALBUM:** *MOTHER OF ALL*, MANEESH DE MOOR.

Truly letting go, deeper into the dream

As Mei's mind searched for logic, her feelings told her to relax further and calmly listen.

The sparkling energy in the water continued to speak soothingly to her: 'It's time to surrender what you have been taught up until now; the way of that tribe is not your path of peace. You came to Gaia in answer to the call of beautiful and new creativity – you had no intent to entertain fear or power over others. We are benevolent guides, here as agreed to remind you to transcend all fear through embodying a natural state of freedom within your body. To begin with, please carefully step under the waterfall, breathe slowly and deeply to surrender and relax.'

Mei tentatively stepped into the rock pool and walked carefully across to stand under the rushing water. She shivered as the cool water poured onto the crown of her head and down her body. Every time her mind said enough, the sparkling energy told her to enter the timelessness – to breathe slowly and deeply and let go even more. Mei became entranced into tranquility as the negative voice in her head dissolved with the sound of the rushing water. She felt her awareness moving beyond time and space into nothingness, she closed her eyes and with a deep sigh of relief completely let go. As all tension in her body dissolved, she felt an ecstatic surge of energy refresh every cell in her being and incredible joy and love ... the bliss of timelessness and boundlessness.

When she came out from under the water, Mei found fresh fruit floating in the stream. After eating the fruit and drinking some water, she rested in the warm cave, enjoying the filtered golden sunlight.

÷

A practice of letting go: organise a personal journey into nature, make sure you take plenty of nourishment and clothing options for different weather. When you get to your chosen destination settle in, sit quietly, journal, contemplate, sit by water or under a large tree dreaming, eat, dance, sing, explore, swim, sunbathe. Simply relax and let go of everything outside of the time you spend there with the nature spirits and divine elementals.

SONG: 'ALL MY LIFE IS A CEREMONY' (MOSE REMIX), MOSE AND DOE PAORO.

IT'S TIME FOR NEW
CREATION STORIES
OF LOVE, BEAUTY,
HARMONY AND
UNITY.

Bridging the dream into true divine nature

Day by day, week by week, month by month, Mei was guided to wake just before the sun, go into the valley for a walk, and move, stretch and strengthen her body. She gathered fresh fruit, nuts, roots, edible flowers and leafy greens, then returned and stood under the waterfall. The meals she began to intuitively make from the seasonal bounty were refreshing and deeply nourishing. Mei lost her sense of time, and simply felt a strong sense of belonging to the boundless beauty and harmony all around her in the magnificent valley. If she ever had regretful or fearful thoughts, her feelings guided her to come back to enjoying herself and become really clear about what she was wanting.

'Stay focused upon yourself and committed to refreshing and renewing to the purity of your true-self' spoke the sparkling energy in the waterfall.

Mei cherished her deeper awareness; her senses had become finely attuned to finding pleasure and joy in the most fragrant flowers, the sweetest fruit, the most beautiful vistas, hearing every sound and knowing just what to do next. In becoming one with her true divine nature, she became highly attuned to the natural world all around her.

One morning, the fragrance of ripe mangos led Mei to a large mango tree that she had not visited for a while. She stretched up to the large limbs and climbed with satisfying strength and agility up to where the branches forked out and effortlessly contemplated adventuring out from the valley. She was shown a vision of a canoe on a beach, and as she felt a full body 'yes', became eager to journey to enjoy what was next.

✣

Self-enquire: how do you creatively express your true divine nature? From this reflection enter into dreaming with the suggested song and then journal any insights or inspiration. Can you bridge anything from your dream into your life now that would be beneficial and refreshingly new? Is there a change to your life that you have been wanting to make that this prompts you to address?

SONG: 'RAISE YOUR VOICE'.
ALBUM: *MEDICINE WOMAN*, MOSE AND SUYANA.

Future visions

Early in the morning, Mei headed north out of the valley, following a stream of water with the sparkling energy flowing along with her. She felt like she was in a completely new world, discovering many beautiful new birds and flowers. By the afternoon, she could hear the ocean and by dusk reached a small beach in a protected inlet.

Mei was absolutely joyous to be by the ocean again. In a protected cove, where fresh water trickled into the sea, she set herself up in a rock cave and watched the sky change from pale blue to the softest pinks fading into indigo.

Just before the sun began to rise in the morning, Mei ran to swim in the ocean and was greeted by a pod of dolphins. They played together catching waves and floating joyously in the warm turquoise water. When Mei came back to the beach, she discovered a washed up canoe – just like in her vision. When she looked in the canoe, she discovered wood carving tools and was given another vision of the canoe made into a long shape with a fin. A flash of light in the water caught her eye and she went down to the water's edge – staring into the crystalline waves she received a vision of riding on top of the waves on a long board of wood. She laughed as it seemed like such fun.

Mei contemplated the inspiration for some time before she decided to carve the canoe. She listened to the stories held in the wood as she gently carved for many moons. She completed the longboard by slotting a dolphin-inspired fin into the base.

✢

Begin a habit of making a note or quick sketch of any vision that presents an unexpected yet interesting idea during your day. When time presents, sit down, relaxing through gentle breathing and open your imagination as you look at the note or sketch, allow yourself to playfully explore the idea and see its unknown relevance or potential. Write or sketch any interesting information or ideas into your creative journal. Let the idea take you where it has energy.

SONG: 'INTO THE DEEP BLUE'.
ALBUM: *GALIM*, **LEMON AND SOUL AND GIL HADASH.**

They always knew in their
hearts that they were made for
bliss and no one could ever
convince them otherwise.

Catching waves

Mei sat by the ocean with her longboard, just watching the waves, and contemplating the wisdom and inspiration offered by the sparkling energy.

She took her board to the shoreline every morning for many more moons, practising moving her body on the board, and then quietly stretched, allowing harmony and flexibility into her mind and body.

One morning she felt a fluid receptivity to taking the board further into the water. Mei never rushed anything, without forcing or pushing she was harmoniously patient and peaceful within herself. Mei felt a rush of ecstatic joy, and as she paddled across the water, a pod of dolphins joined her and guided her out to catch the long rolling waves. She squealed with pure delight as she stood on her board, moving gracefully around to create momentum – it was the most fun she'd ever experienced and felt this potential had drawn her to Gaia.

Mei's daily ritual became practising the art of surfing and joyously appreciating and caring for herself. Mei glowed with a luminous radiance – she embodied pure joy and creative vitality, living her true divine nature.

One afternoon the bay became very still; the water looked like liquid mother of pearl. Mei sat on her longboard floating quietly, just watching and listening. She heard someone singing and then saw a man in a canoe coming into the bay. Mei felt great excitement rush through her body – could it be Maleko?

The sparkling energy in the water said: 'Yes, it is your beloved.'

Once reunited, Mei shared the joy of riding waves with Maleko. She knew they would continue to live harmoniously together, experimenting newly and refining the art of surfing.

As they courageously followed their bliss, they became the first surfers.

✦

Remind yourself what feels personally blissful; write this as a list into your journal. Close your eyes and imagine the personally blissful activities turned into pure energy expressed as gentle waves in a pearlescent ocean. Imagine yourself paddling out on a longboard and catching the energy of pure bliss one wave after the other; see yourself being carried by the light of what feels good to you, welcoming more to come.

SONG: 'PLANTAS SAGRADAS'.
ALBUM: *FAMILIA*, NICK BARBACHANO.

Frangipani dreaming

Who were the first surfers? Do we really know the whole story? Perhaps the first surfers became so relaxed and fully present in their earthly bodies that they completely spiritualised, continuing to live with Gaia in an eternal bliss. Playfully imagine this as true as you enter into this dreamscape.

✦

Olivia's personal practice of mindful movement and letting go grew stronger every year; with every breath of release, she untangled her mind to be free from suffering. The sweetness of her unfurling was the only thing she held – albeit tenderly. Privately and beyond words, the whole process of her self-integration was quite mysterious. She felt more youthful everyday becoming charged with the creative power of weaving her own story by golden thoughts.

After deliberately dreaming of adventure for quite some time, the opportunity to travel effortlessly fell into place. She booked a trip to a romantically wild, hidden destination, not visible on Google Maps, but she'd been told by a friend of a friend it was completely divine.

Landing at a tiny airport she was greeted with leis of frangipani and the kind of humidity that demands slow motion. The pure joy of frangipani was even more beautiful than she had imagined.

At the wharf she excitedly chartered a small boat to island hop to her destination. Her tour guide warmly helped her onboard and as they headed out across the brilliant turquoise ocean, time seemed to dissolve along with any phone reception. Mesmerised by the vastness and immense beauty, she soaked in her feelings of freedom and excited anticipation.

She arrived at her destination to meet exquisitely beautiful local people known as the Gaians. A small group of them were resting in the shade beneath large palm trees, their surfboards were laying on the grass covered in fallen frangipanis. As Olivia entered the portal of this certain paradise she is met with a warm greeting, an intoxicatingly relaxing wave of energy washed over her, bringing a deeper sense of truly belonging to earth in her present here and now.

A beautiful young woman smiled and invited Olivia to join them: 'Hello dear friend, I am Mei, welcome to the divine bliss of Gaia.'

**SONG: 'SOMEWHERE OVER THE RAINBOW/WHAT A WONDERFUL WORLD'.
ALBUM: *FACING FUTURE*, ISRAEL KAMAKAWIWO'OLE.**

I am the new one

Keeping your eyes closed, breathe gently and effortlessly, calming the mind into a meditative, dreamy state. Begin with imagining a blissful scenario, allow yourself to fully fantasise, linger over every little detail, enjoy the deliciousness of every aspect. This can be a scenario that you would like to experience on this day or further in the future. To assist you enjoying and relaxing into your dreamy imagining, you may like to play music or burn incense. Completely relax your body and mind as you continue to cultivate feelings of appreciation and enthusiasm. Open your eyes gently, and journal any inspiration.

'Ahhhh, everything is so beautiful, my life is overflowing with beauty.
I smile to myself, I thank my body.
I am enough, I have enough and I happily receive the surprises
and gifts that come each day, I move forward mindfully aware.
I dream of paradise and wonder what deliciousness is coming,
I know I am worthy to receive the life of my dreams.
I let go and joyfully relax into a brand new day.
I am the new one, I embody innocence and grace.'

———

SONG: 'ANCESTRAL BLESSINGS'.
ALBUM: *SAMA*, MANEESH DE MOOR.

Seer of
paradise

You are prosperity, you are the beloved,
you didn't come to earth to think like a beggar.
Do not forget your supreme true-self.
What could you seek that you cannot be?
You are free to live through eternal presence.
What do you truly desire?
Are you nearly done or always before completion?

÷

Listen to your silent breathing -
you know how to embody your truth and beauty.
Welcome eternal unfurling of the inner lotuses,
have no resistance to freshness.
Let go and relax as everything comes into balance.
Enjoy the pleasure of your own sweet nectar,
let it permeate your whole being.
Allow yourself to shiver with delight -
tremble and shake with ecstasy.
Celebrate life – drink it in.
Enjoy the freshness of contentment,
let go of anything that makes you hungry.
Do not seek the comfort of mundane illusions.
Let go and know what it is you truly desire.
Desire is your power to create anew.
Imagine your paradise, then relax, let everything go,
allow what you are wanting to come,
have no resistance to exquisiteness.

———

SONG: 'MACHI'.
ALBUM: *FOUR GREAT WINDS*, PEIA.

Enter the dreams of Seers, releasing the knots of the not-self

The Seer travels through the mind's eye, also known as the blue orb of the third-eye, to see the gold of life. They can fearlessly traverse their inner worlds and into other worldly realms as they behold the sword of truth and the FLAME OF COMPASSION. As Seers go deeper into their own truth, they uncover hidden aspects of self and bring them into the light with full self-acceptance, humour and honour. In this ongoing process of integration one reimagines the self and reclaims totality with the holy gold of self-illumination – divine compassion.

Seers do not enter into a shamanic quest. They do not seek to recover or retrieve a person's soul stories that have been left to shame or abandoned due to corruption, they go into the inner worlds for themselves in search of gold. Seers are not looking for what is wrong, drama or sympathy, they take their light of compassion, truth, joy and love to invite all life to follow the natural way into the light of bliss. Seers become very clear about their purpose due to their ability to ask the right questions; they willingly play their part as it becomes self-evident thereby activating matter and subtle energy to create beautiful new fractal patterns, expressed as new ways of living.

Seers are magicians who untie the knots of lies that entangle oneself to an embodiment of the not-self. Seers understand that our ancestors live within and any light they bring to any moment in time, past, present or future, illuminates greater potential for seven generations back and forth through the ancestral line. Seers enter stories from different angles and may be perceived as an angel: a subtle energy form who brings the light of compassion and truth to a situation shrouded in darkness and confusion. Seers understand that the past, present and future can be accessed through the unified field of the dreamer who is willing to see the light of truth and wields the capacity to retell a story with unity consciousness for healing and resolution.

✧

Sit comfortably, close your eyes and look up into the space between your eyes. You can also direct your eyes through this space to the back of your skull. Patiently practise this exercise until you see a golf-ball size indigo-blue orb. Explore going through this inner portal with pure intentions.

——

SONG: 'OM – THIRD EYE CHAKRA – INNER KNOWING', 432HZ CHAKRA SUITE, VOL II: SACRED SOUNDS, FLOAT WAVES AND DOE PAORO.

The dream to know thy self

Enter these dreamscapes, practise being Seer, can you see yourself dreaming?

✧

As Ava began studying qigong* and going deeper into the practice, becoming softer and stronger, every cell of her being was becoming enlightened.

Her teacher spoke of the philosophy: 'This practice will cultivate gentle and present mind focus. It is ancient yet so relevant to our modern life, a way to balance the body and support health and longevity as well as building qi or vital energy. In our practice we work to empty our mind, be formless and cultivate a genuine smile that is both inward and outward. We move like water, the mother of all life: creative, shapeless, adaptive, strong yet fluid. Pour water into a cup it becomes the cup, pour water into a teapot, it becomes the teapot. We move like bamboo, a symbol of strength, flexibility and growth; the higher it grows,

the deeper it bows. Bamboo is hollow on the inside – it grows quite simply. This reminds us that we should keep an open mind, stay open to all possibilities of exploration and growth.'

Everything about Ava was changing; one thing led to another, she let go of so many things, some suddenly, others incrementally. She moved with more grace and ease, changed the way she felt about her body and how she dressed. As her nervous system relaxed, all chatter and moody silences disappeared; she smiled more and laughed a lot. As Ava's mind cleared, she made better decisions, no longer entertaining suffering.

Ava became increasingly curious about the beautiful woman in the painting on the wall of the qigong studio. The subject was indeed a mystery. She found that the portrait had been painted in 770 BCE, and she translated what was written on the artwork into English for contemplation.

I am the spirit of liberty, I could have been Empress of the great lands – I chose the path of the new one and became Amrita.

Listen to the song below, enter a dream of wonder ... who might you be beyond what you know now? Journal and contemplate anything inspiring.

———

SONG: 'SONG OF GRATITUDE'.
ALBUM: *LIQUID SILK*, MARINA RAY.

*Qigong can be described as a mind-body-spirit practice for more energy and less stress, improving one's mental and physical health by integrating posture, movement, breathing technique, self-massage, sound and focused intent.

Green Tara Mantra

Om Tāre Tuttāre Ture Svāhā

OM! O Tara! I entreat you, O Tara! O swift one! Hail!
Om Tāre Tuttāre Ture Svāhā
Tara, whose name means 'star' or 'she who ferries across'
is a Bodhisattva* of compassion, always before completion.
Green Tara refreshingly liberates clarity of intention.
She represents compassion in action, she is both resting
upon her lotus and diving into the mud of existence to stir
the desire to be joyously alive - she awakens the world
from the hypnosis of entropy and the mundane.
Green Tara is pure, clean, honest, beautiful, inspiring, joyously thankful, unified and eternal.
Om Tāre Tuttāre Ture Svāhā
Om Tara Tu Tara Tu Ray Swaha
Om Tāre Tuttāre Ture Svāhā
Om Tāre Tuttāre Ture Svāhā
Om Tāre Tuttāre Ture Svāhā
Om Tāre Tuttāre Ture Svāhā
Om Tāre Tuttāre Ture Svāhā
Om Tāre Tuttāre Ture Svāhā
Om Tāre Tuttāre Ture Svāhā
Om Tāre Tuttāre Ture Svāhā

Work with this mantra if it resonates and
ongoing if guided.

———

SONG: 'OM TARE TUTTARE TURE SOHA'.
ALBUM: *INNER PEACE*, ANI CHOYING DROLMA.

**Bodhisattva is a sanskrit word that translates as an individual who embodies their
siddhis, relating to all others with great compassion, reverence and grace.*

Dreaming of Amrita

After class Ava loved to sip tea in the studio's courtyard garden under a cherry blossom tree. The warm spring sun shone upon the fragrant tree which was in full blossom, buzzing with bees, petals falling everywhere like confetti.

As Ava sat looking into the pond, she saw something move beneath the surface and presumed the luminous green was some kind of fish. Watching the water for another glimpse, she saw two bright green eyes looking at her. She sensed that she was being invited to ask the water creature a question.

With amusement she playfully responded: 'Could you tell me more about Amrita?' The creature began swaying and she thought to herself that it looked like some kind of a dragon.

'Yes, I am the green water dragon – close your eyes please.' Ava closed her eyes with a whimsical curiosity. The green water dragon continued: 'Take audible inhales and exhales and listen to the sound of your breath.' Ava followed the instructions. 'Now breathe without a sound and keep listening for your breath.' Ava obliged and was amazed as all mind chatter disappeared into silence; she could sense the green water dragon was speaking through her heart. 'Look at the space between your eyebrows and watch for an indigo orb.' As Ava observed that space, an indigo orb appeared and grew larger. 'Relax, allow your imagination to open and bring an answer to your question, enjoy!' A vision of Amrita appeared in Ava's mind's eye, a vivid story unfolding like a beautiful film beginning with a young woman named Lian.

✦

Strengthening your imagination when there is no urgent requirement for a resolution trains your mind to look beyond obvious solutions for everyday problems. Spiritual fitness and command of the mind are key to responding swiftly with grace, without pulling focus and momentum away from that which you are truly wanting, when facing day-to-day challenges. Being able to perceive new resolutions from a broader perspective is an invaluable strength. Practise opening your imagination to perceive Amrita's story by activating your third eye in meditation as previously described, and journal your insights.

SONG: 'SONG FOR A PURE HEART',
ALBUM: *IN LIGHT*, MEI-LAN.

Rice paper love letters dream

Weave the golden thread of innocence, grace and compassion through your own stories. Remember you may retell any past event in the light of your own loving compassion to bring healing through all time and space.

÷

They first met in the fields outside the village. When Lian turned thirteen, she secretly left the palace grounds to explore the province. In her wandering she met a much older, charming adventurer practised in the art of seduction. He told her his family would never allow him to marry into Lian's family dynasty, insisting they could only secretly rendezvous. He came and went just enough to create a desire she believed only he could satisfy. He never stayed long enough to be truly known, preferring to appear as a worldly, grand warrior. He wrote her letters claiming she was the most beautiful young woman in the whole world; she saved every one in a beautifully carved red sandalwood box. Lian loved to fantasise about him, but through this state of distraction and self-deception, she lost true perception of herself. When he returned, albeit very briefly, she was hypnotised by his presence, easily collapsing into submission and doing everything she could to please him.

One spring day Lian sat in the warm sun on her bedroom balcony reading his letters. She didn't expect him to return for many moons and although confused upon hearing his voice at the gates, immediately assumed he had come to publicly declare his love. She stood up to wave and saw her family greeting him and a female companion. She gasped as she saw the young woman with him was her beautiful cousin. All of a sudden a spring shower burst; she stood in the rain watching his love letters dissolve.

÷

Choose a significant event from your life and retell it with a completely different outcome from what happened at that time, and write your retelling in your journal. Contemplate what you have written and then imagine well into the future based on your retelling – what might the effect be? Write about your perceptions. Refine your storytelling until it is exactly what you desire.

SONG: 'GAJUMARU'.
ALBUM: *PELLUCIDITY*, YAIMA.

In moments of intensity may you remain aware
of your freedom to enjoy breathing,
choose your own good feeling thoughts and be
aligned in communion with relaxed inner greatness.

Dream of true perception

As festivities were being organised to welcome the cousin and her fiancée, Lian began to settle into her body and acknowledge illusions. She could see she'd ignored her intuition though her hunger for validation, leaving herself open to seduction. Rather than think badly of herself or others, she knew in her heart any problem was an opportunity to gain inner strength by moving through it like water, bowing to it like bamboo. She chose to honestly and humbly acknowledge how she had betrayed herself, bow in reverence to herself and draw all focus upon realigning with her inner greatness.

A servant came and instructed Lian to get ready to join the family. Lian went to the bath house and sat quietly in the warm tub staring at a painting of the beautiful Green Tara. She enquired what to do in light of this situation and sensed it beneficial to give herself some space to hear an answer.

As Lian dressed she was guided to gather flowers for her hair. She went to the fragrant gardens by the lotus pools and picked blossoms, then sat by the still water threading them into her hair. She sighed upon seeing her sorrowful face in the pool's reflection, then she noticed a luminous creature moving beneath the surface that looked like a small dragon.

The green water dragon stared into her eyes and spoke into her heart: 'You must forget who you thought you were, that sad face doesn't belong to you, it is a mask you are choosing to wear. Close your eyes, meditate as you have been taught – listen to your silent breathing, quieten your mind for divine inspiration to come.'

Lian appreciated the guidance, and as she sat quietly breathing in meditation, an inner vision appeared. It was Green Tara beckoning her to enter a mountain temple through large ornate doors.

✢

A breathing practice to calm your mind. Breath audibly through your nose by gently restricting the flow of air through your throat; this is often referred to as the ocean breath. After a while breathe silently but keep listening for your breath. Observe how your mind silences as it plays the game of listening to that which it cannot hear but knows is there.

SONG: 'EAST OF THE FULL MOON', DEUTER.

Dive deeper into the dream

Green Tara was dancing around the high mountain temple when Lian entered through the southern doors of the elegant open air space. An altar was straight before her on the north side, the east and west sides were open to the sky and distant mountains, and fine white mist swept across the floor like rolling waves. There was an energy of incredible clarity inside the space, everything in the interior glowed. The floor was a luminous green; pale pink lotuses grew from a mirror-like pool of water inset in the floor before the altar. A soft waterfall of ultra-fine gold dust fell behind the altar of one hundred lit candles in golden, lotus-shaped cups.

Green Tara came over to Lian and kissed her on the cheek, laughing and smiling through her brilliant green eyes. 'I'm so glad you have come. Welcome fellow water dragon – we are the luminous ones destined to create heaven on earth. You like to play don't you? I want you to remember, I encourage you to let go of your seriousness and enter pure adventure. You liked my portrait painting and yet, that is only one story. I am timelessness, I am boundlessness, I am bliss, I am the spirit of liberation animating life. Your desires are the most powerful thing, what you strongly desire will come to you, so be very clear about what you are wanting. If you want to create heaven on earth, you must not limit yourself. Let go of your identity, let go of who they said you should or might be. Ask what is your path to your full creative aliveness?'

Green Tara guided Lian across the floor to the altar. 'Sit here with me my beloved, open your third eye, the incredible portals of your DNA. You will know, you are free to see beyond space and time.' They sat down together on green velvet cushions before the altar and closed their eyes.

✧

Recall an occurrence in your life that had mystical qualities, something that was unexplainable, and write about it in your journal. Recall a very normal occurrence and write about that too. How do these perceptions differ? Contemplate if there's something mysterious in the normal occurrence that you haven't yet perceived? Write your musings in your journal.

**SONG: 'OM KUMARA MANTRA (INNOCENCE)'.
ALBUM: *A DEEPER LIGHT*, DEVA PREMAL AND MITTEN WITH MANOSE.**

Travelling north in dreams

In meditation with Green Tara, Lian was shown four directions.

LAND OF THE SETTING SUN

The sun was setting to the west of a beautiful valley, in the last light, smoke could be seen coming from little villages. An army of warriors on black horses raced across the land shouting 'Victory'. In a distant palace servants rushed around to meet the demands of a dissatisfied, old empress who stood at a window watching the sky become dark.

LAND OF THE RISING SUN

The sun began to rise in the east, shining upon great beauty where people harmoniously began their day together, each attending to each other, garden and home with great devotion and appreciation. The freshest food was being prepared, children played freely, every detail of care flowed into an abundant, shared life full of creative innovation.

POWER TO TRANSFORM

A snake moved through the grass in the south, silently shedding its skin, with clear eyes it proficiently let go of its old self. Never looking back it slithered away gracefully, its body shimmering with the freshness and strength of unified beauty.

UNKNOWN SWEETNESS

Lian saw a radiant woman standing facing north on a mountain, the sky was extremely clear and a magnificent view could be seen in all directions. The mountains spoke: 'We bless you to flow as Amrita, the elixir of life.'

✤

Lian slowly opened her eyes, knowing what she desired – a vision of herself as Amrita was beginning to flow. She made the decision to bridge her dream walk towards becoming Amrita.

✤

Enter a dream space with the intention to travel towards your north star, and journal your visions. Contemplate if you desire to bridge anything from that dream into your life.

SONG: 'WINDS OF CHANGE'.
ALBUM: *BLISSFUL JOURNEY*, MARINA RAYE.

Dream of the beloved's temple

Lian's eyes were no longer perceiving with hunger, they had become ignited with the true flame of eternal liberty. She was ready to be fully awake as the beloved-self; she no longer desired approval from others. As she walked back to the palace, her insights became crystal clear.

Raucous noise filled the dining room and upon hearing the drunken celebrations, her inner sense of knowing affirmed it was a good time to leave. She quietly went to her room, packed a bag of belongings and without looking back, went to the stables. She saddled her horse, discreetly left the grounds and rode into the night. Lian stopped to rest in the secret grotto where she had spent many hours with her former lover – she felt a deep relief and appreciation for being awakened to true adventure. Without regret she felt excited for what was to come.

After weeks of discreet travel, Lian came to an empty mountain temple. She entered and immediately knew she could breathe beauty and harmony into the dusty space. The views were magnificent, there were rooms to live in and a large ceremonial space led onto a balcony with large, carved stone dragons at each side. An old garden nestled around the temple would be perfect to grow food and fragrance.

After many moons of transformation, the nectar of life flowed through every cell in Lian's body. She cultivated a deep connection with the spirit of the mountains and the serpent ley lines*, and small rose quartz crystals appeared in a distinctive pattern on a plateau in the temple grounds. As she playfully moved around the crystal grid she downloaded a sacred qi** dance, a fluid movement sequence for complete wellbeing.

In meditation Green Tara celebrated and affirmed she had received this timeless gift as cosmically intended.

As Lian became Amrita, the inspiring spirit of liberty, she drew beloveds through time and space to join her in harmonious and exquisite co-creativity.

✣

Dance with true abandon to the song below – let energy pour through you.

SONG: 'THE GREAT LIVING LIBRARY' (JAKARE REMIX), DEYA DOVA.

*Serpent ley lines carry the spiritual life force of Gaia around the planet.
**Qi – vital energy or life force that keeps a person's spiritual, emotional, mental and physical health in balance.

Bridging the dream
into a real adventure

A soft breeze stirred through the courtyard garden and cherry blossoms fell upon Ava's face. Ava became aware of her body as the vision of Amrita faded into mists of the great mountains. In the gentle meditation, the lotus of liberation had opened and released the sweetness of Amrita to move freely through Ava's memory palaces, illuminating inspiration and clearing her psyche of any myths or stories that may limit.

Every time Ava meditated, the nectar of Amrita flowed bringing new visions of beauty and harmony, stirring Ava's imagination to rise from the muddiness of entropy and self-doubt. With the sweetness of beginning to sense her true-self, Ava was encouraged to honestly admit what her heart truly desired – thereby surrendering any resistance to believing her true desires could be real. Magic happened as her true perception opened, revealing amazing opportunities and fruitful propositions. In acknowledging a strong desire for new adventure, Ava was offered an opportunity to travel to a remote area in the Himalayas for qigong teacher training.

Ava arrived the day before her training commenced to spend time acclimatising to the elevated location. She wandered the tiny paths around the mountain village and discovered a radiant temple set amongst magical gardens. At the entrance she stopped, recalling a vision from meditation, and exclaiming in amazement, 'Amrita's temple?'

A beautiful and luminous woman came out to greet her, beckoning her to enter the sweetly infinite realm beyond time and space. Ava's life continued to unfold in miraculous ways since she'd opened every cell in her body to the sacred golden nectar of life.

÷

From this part of the dream story open your imagination, write another sequence, create art, poetry or a different story in your journal.

SONG: 'MAMAHEY', MOSE AND MUTA.

The Seers

Imagine this archetype rising within our culture and self-enquire if you are called to explore and embody any aspect.

÷

To be Seer is to live without any self-repression and a very broad perspective. If you have the pleasure of meeting a Seer, your own good feeling thoughts and light-hearted perspective has attracted very beautiful and graceful company.

Even though the clearer sense of knowing we are born with may dissipate through impressions made by the limiting beliefs of others, omnipresent evolutionary forces will always support awakening. Growing up in a world functioning on limiting beliefs activates a strong desire to discover a broader perspective in individuals who are destined to become Seers. These individuals possess a strong DIVINE TRUE WILL to succeed in moving through the distraction of suffering in order to uphold clarity for themselves and others.

Seers are orientated to self-activating their imaginations, to see through any limiting fears and illuminate all possibilities in life. They choose to focus on life, undisturbed or hypnotised by cultural concepts of death, knowing that life goes on always before completion, either physical or non-physical.

Seers are devoted to self-mastery in order to illuminate brilliant ideas for great benefit. Being around a Seer is like have all your very personal bells rung by the illumination of any hidden gifts, talents and secret true-self dreams.

Seers have no interest in being saviours or to forsake themselves for popularity, their take-it-or-leave-it attitude affords them the freedom to endlessly adventure through life with a light heart.

Seers never look back with regret or into the future with fear. Their clear and incorruptible sense of self-knowing elevates them beyond hunger, impatience, entropy, disorientation, confusion and distraction.

Seers are brilliant, free at heart, joyously appreciative of everything and unapologetically glowing, with luminous wellbeing.

Dragon dancing, phoenix rising

You will know without doubt when you are ready to enter the portal of personal joy that is the practice of qigong. You will easily find wonderful teachers and guides of qigong practice upon the journey of finding yourself at home in your body with a deep sense of physical and mental relief. You may ask yourself why this wonderful practice has been so well hidden in the plain light of day? You will know the answer as soon as you begin to practice – the rising power of true warmth and surrender to greater love within you as a result of the qigong practice empowers you beyond programmed limitations.

As you are freed from any form of self-harm, you live beautifully with grace and simplicity, capable of remaining connected to the rhythms of earth and your own true divine nature, never having the impulse to seek quick fixes or distractions that numb you to feeling the depth of who you truly are. Your genuine smile gives you the power to truly feel life and allow it to pour through you.

I exist in a luminous place of pure awareness.
The truth I see is living in me.
I am Seer in grace beyond time and place.
I allow energy to move effortlessly through my body,
without resistance to dissolving belief one needs to suffer.
I transform all with the truth of liberty
that exists within my heart.
I am Seer in timelessness. I am Seer in boundlessness.
I am Seer in beauty. I am Seer in unity.
I am Seer in harmony. I am Seer in exquisiteness.
I am Seer in bliss as I surrender any holding on to fear,
I release all regret and shame.
My sense of knowing who I am in truth is clear and eternal.
My greater truth is seen through feeling the deepest appreciation.

Flame
SONGS of
paradise

It is wise to imagine everything about your personal
experience is improving if that is what you desire.

It is wise to listen to and sing the song in your heart,
and only think about things that feel good to you
if you are wanting to enjoy and relax into
receiving the life of your dreams.

Allow yourself to enjoy your own dreams,
linger upon them, delight in their evolving.

Be easy on yourself, gently breathe in freshness
and hum with appreciation.

As she listened to dusk's serenity:
crickets chirping, gentle water trickling,
flowers closing, moths fluttering with the rising moon,
she felt great relief and the pure joy of simply being in her heart,
she lay in a deep trance with the sweet sounds of life
she surrendered to life's sweet love song and
appreciated every delicious note as it played
over and over with ever-increasingexquisite beauty and harmony.

Enter here into the dream songs of whispering flames

As you enter these dreamscapes, can you hear the golden song – the whispering flames of loving kindness, truth, understanding, courage all softly harmonised with a willingness to listen?

✢

He was standing in the shadows of the large olive tree planted central to the courtyard, and he spoke with the warmth of a deeply fragrant, slow burning candle – arousing a desire for more.

'In all honesty, I am not hungry anymore, this is different, life has become sweeter and very fulfilling, so yes, I am looking forward to this unfolding, it will be pure adventure. Yes. Thank you. Be well my friend.' As he put the phone in his pocket he noticed her and gave a gentle smile.

Ti could just make out his face, his eyes shining like the moonlit sea at night. He turned and left via the ornately carved wooden gate. She didn't know who he was, but she was deeply intrigued – it had been a night of many layers.

She decided to follow his cue and left via the garden exit. When she got into her car it smelt of alcohol and women's fragrance; she noticed her boyfriend's jacket on the back seat and recalled how their evening had begun. They were meant to attend the gathering together, yet he was very drunk when she picked him up from his work, so she took him to his place instead.

Ti decided it was time to face her discomfort and do something about the root cause. She started driving towards her home, opening the window, enjoying the soft breeze, consciously clearing every negative thought with long exhales. She knew there was no point in negative self-talk or looking for the first stitch in the fabric of her own suffering – it was time to courageously choose better feeling thoughts and free the song in her true-self's heart.

✢

Contemplate the simple decisions you make daily about tasks you do, like how you shower; imagine doing this task entirely differently by infusing every detail with the song of your heart's joy and enthusiasm. If inspired bridge this imagined experience into your life for a refreshing change.

SONG: 'RAINBOW STARDUST', MOSE AND ELIH.

Relationship harmony can only be realised
when freedom is allowed
freedom to live as an expression
of the true undivided self.
freedom to find one's own natural rhythm
through the seasons, freedom to follow personal bliss.

History is irrelevant to bliss.

Freedom can only be given to oneself as no one can
free any other from choosing the disharmonious
thoughts that limit one's true freedom.

Refreshing dreams

Ti drove into the mountains to spend the day near her favourite waterfall. She nestled in a private nook, and as the sun gently shone through the watery mists she felt calmness wash over her. For most of the day she contemplated her life, thinking about what she truly desired, and what true freedom really was. The sound of the rushing water felt soothing and clearing as she breathed slowly, focusing her attention on her lower dantian*.

Ti reflected upon when she was fourteen and first lived in France as an exchange student. The initial experience was profoundly heart opening – everything about the place and culture deeply awakened her true divine sensual nature. Ti had entered a very innocent and beautiful relationship with another girl; it seemed very natural to explore intimacy, sensuality and sexuality together. They found a secluded sanctuary in the forest near their village to enjoy their intimate adventure. One warm summer day as they lay naked in each other's arms, eye gazing with deep appreciation, students from their school discovered them. Everything changed from that moment as shame,

guilt, gossip, secrecy and power games seeped into every aspect of their lives. Ti's fragile pubescent self-identity and feminine sensuality was deeply disturbed, patterns of self-denial manifesting as a repression of natural expression.

As the sun started to drop to the west, Ti undressed and jumped into the water – squealing with the coldness and laughing as she playfully swam around. She floated, looking up at the clouds and the endless blue sky declaring, 'I am free to choose, I am free to let go!'

She climbed out of the water shivering with the electricity of transformation. As Ti freed herself from self-judgment, embracing a new compassionate perspective with deep appreciation for her innocence, she unlocked something deep inside her heart, feeling refreshed and deeply relieved. Instead of listening to fear Ti was listening to her own source of inner wisdom.

⁕

Enter a dream space while gently humming to yourself. Allow all feelings to arise as you embrace yourself with warmth, acceptance and loving kindness.

SONG: 'ASATOMA', SAM GARRETT AND MOLLIE MENDOZA.

*Dantian, or dan tian, translates from Chinese to mean 'field of elixir'. Known as the vessel of jing, the lower dantian is a focal point for transmutation of one of the three treasures, or essences, vital to a person's health.

The upper dantian
Heaven abides and therefore you are here.
Your heart-community-mind wants to speak silently,
listen through your emptiness.
See through the illusion of separation,
there is nothing stopping you from
bringing heaven to earth.
Your intentions, perceptions and imagination
sings life into being.

+

The middle dantian
Be unconditional, don't hold your heart
hostage to any demands of the not-self.
If you want happiness, remove the want,
the purity of heart simply is.
Follow your heart, become your bliss.
True-self, heart-centred creature of earth.

+

The lower dantian
Be at peace with where you are, nowhere else is better.
You are the juice - the elixir.
You are the orgasmic presence and the lover.
You are the ecstasy that you know.
You have no beginning and no end
and yet you are beginnings and endings
always before completion -
Celebrate that!
Liberty is your name.

DO NOT DISTURB THE DELICATE
PROCESS OF CREATION WITH
DOUBT OR CRITICISM.
ALLOW THE NEW EXPERIENCE
OF LIFE BE YOURS TO
REALISE AS YOU STAY IN
APPRECIATION OF WHAT IS.
LET THE SACRED SONG
OF THE HEART
BE SUNG TO LIFE.

Dreams of sensual self-romance

Ti woke up early feeling like simplifying her wardrobe of clothes and started with cleaning out her drawers. She put on her very favourite Lover's Playlist and began clearing. Each song inspiring her to surrender more to her sensual nature.

When she opened her lingerie drawer she paused at a silk bag, opened it and took out her favourite self-pleasure tool, with the word passion embossed in elegant gold on the handle. She contemplated upon how self-honesty led her to passion and dishonesty to hungry lust. Visions of her sexual experiences streamed through her memory palaces. Wondering how good her life could become, the back of her neck tingled and her heart fluttered. Ti intuitively closed her eyes and saw visions of her liberated-self in a beautiful garden, rain pouring over her face as she celebrated her own sweetness. Ti decided to let go of all seriousness and over-thinking in favour of focusing on only expanding upon thoughts that would draw great beauty and playfulness. She continued to go through her wardrobe, keeping sensual silhouettes and softer fabrics, clearing out anything that felt disharmonious.

Her mother rang: 'Hello darling, how are you going?'

Ti was silent.

'Are you there Ti?' continued her mother.

Ti politely replied: 'Yes Mama, all good here, how are you?'

'Great, thank you,' started her mother.

Ti interrupted lightly: 'Excuse me Mama, there's someone at the door, I must go, lovely to hear from you, see you soon.'

Ti felt lighter from not sharing the delicate metamorphosis she was witnessing in herself, grateful for the timely knock on the door.

÷

If you feel inspired put on a sensual and soft garment and dance. Feel your innocence rise – do not push away any feelings. Let your inner song of golden creativity flow.

SONG: 'THE DANCE & THE WONDER', SAM GARRETT.

Dreaming from a new song

There are golden opportunities in everything – most things are only partially understood. There is richness in the mud of all relationships. Singing a fresh perspective to light changes everything – this act is often called a miracle.

Some perceive the mother as a spider, a powerful creatress
of life and death, and her beautiful daughters as jewels,
caught like glistening dew on her intricate web.
The wise know the mother is a beautiful mystery.
She is the water in everything, she is the unique essences
of liquid crystalline energy that embellish the web.
She is the web that beholds glittering portals of freedom
at the intersections of life.

Ti opened the door to receive an enormous bunch of pink roses. She sighed as she read the card; it was an apology from her boyfriend. She thought that he would make things a lot easier if he was consistent, and she paused as an uneasy feeling cautioned her mid-thought. She took a deep inhale and sighed out slowly with relief. Choosing to turn her judgements into appreciation led to the clarity to see that she could gracefully dissolve her entanglement with him.

Her phone rang – it was her mother – she let it go.

Her mother sent a message: 'Just confirming you are still coming tonight Ti, could you please let me know?'

Then her sister rang and left a message: 'Can you bring some flowers for the table tonight?'

Ti replied yes to both, smiling with a different perception of divine timing, greatly appreciating the flowers sent by her ex-lover.

As Ti drove to her parent's home that evening, she set an intention to relax and enjoy herself rather trying to please anyone. As she contemplated who she really was her inner knowing told her to just let the song in her heart be played out. Good things were coming to her; be patient and expect the unexpected.

⊹

Listen to your perceptions. Draw a golden thread through your mind to see the most beautiful qualities in everything, yourself included.

SONG: 'BLESSED ARE WE'.
ALBUM: *THE FOUR GREAT WINDS*, PEIA.

Dream of the divine creatress

The empress who seeks control is asking to loose everything.
The divine creatress who lets go of any thoughts that create
distance from ease knows bliss – she who listens to the eternal song
in her heart, rather than the conditioned mind,
can hear love playing in and through everything.

Feeling calm and centred Ti warmly greeted her family and friends, then sat quietly feeling exhilarated by new self-awareness and good intentions. 'I am freedom, I am beauty, I am patient, I am courageous. I relax and deeply appreciate everything, good things are coming to me.'

The gathering grew as more individuals arrived and her parents' home became full of colour and movement.

Ti's father greeted the guy who she'd seen in the courtyard the week before: 'Oh good you're here in time for the meal, everyone this is Tobias.'

Tobias smiled at Ti as he sat in the empty seat next to her.

Ti's mother looked at her with a warm smile. At first impulse Ti imagined she was asking, 'Where's your boyfriend?' Ti softened and took a moment to centre, gazing at her mother as she slowly finished her mouthful. She took a slow breath, as she consciously let go of all projections, her heart open to purely receive her mother's smile.

Ti's mother warmly complimented her: 'You look refreshingly radiant darling, I'm so happy that you are here with us tonight.'

'Thank you,' replied Ti.

Tobias smiled at Ti, and she warmly smiled in return, softly guiding herself to slow down, remain relaxed and observant.

As Ti relaxed more, allowing the evening to effortlessly unfold, she found there was something incredibly innocent and beautiful to appreciate in everyone present. Through her appreciative eyes and open mind, each experiential segment unfurled very exquisitely.

⁜

In a familiar gathering, set an intention to be more observant. Listen keenly to the tone of others voices; soften as you cultivate a deeper warmth from within.

SONG: 'HIGHER THAN THE MOUNTAINS'.
ALBUM: *THE DANCE AND THE WONDER*, SAM GARRETT.

Dream softly,
softly darling

After dining out together, Tobias came back to Ti's place.

Tobias looked at a photo of her parents: 'Your folks are very interesting people, I appreciate being able to reconnect with them.'

'I am really just getting to know them,' Ti responded. 'I spent many years in France studying, first in secondary school followed by a long internship working in haute couture fashion. My parents offered my sisters, Cheri and Soleil, and I the freedom to choose how and what we wanted to learn. I chose to study and live abroad, yet somehow I cultivated a thought that they were happy for me to move out as I was difficult to get along with, but I am wondering if I projected this onto them.' Ti looked down.

Tobias lifted her chin to bring her eyes to meet his, looking directly at her as he softly spoke. 'It seems your parents live by the art of allowing, truly loving and trusting you to find your own way. Our culture tends to tell us that freedom is contrary to relationships and yet the best relationships are full of allowing and celebration of difference.'

Tobias sat down on the floor and continued: 'We grew up when the world was beginning to be flooded with all sorts of information – I watched so much stuff on the internet! Looking back I can see it messed with my innocent spirit. I found all relationships very challenging, until my parents separated and my mum completely changed. She let go of all attempts to control others and became beautifully softer; it was very inspiring to see her turn the situation into a blessing. She became so light and warm, like a candle, by being so free spirited and loving she guided us all to relax and get on with enjoying our lives. I asked how she had forgiven my father and she said there was nothing to forgive, history is irrelevant to bliss and life is meant to be pure bliss. Can I put on some music?' added Tobias.

'Certainly,' answered Ti, taking off her shoes to rub her feet.

Take a foot bath and massage your feet thoroughly with sweet smelling oils and/or give this divine experience to a beloved.

SONG: 'KINDRED SPIRIT'
ALBUM: *KOYASAN*: REIKI SOUND HEALING, DEUTER.

*Your essence is listening
to your life-affirming
promises. Your unbound
true-self communicates to
its physical-self with
clear messages sent
through the body via
the chakra flowers –
the subtle energy centres.
The throat chakra is the
energy centre of truth,
you can attune to your
own truth by listening to
how energy sounds and
feels as it moves through
the region of your throat.
The only work you have
to do is honour what
personally feels good.
There is no need to think
about what feels good,
listen to the texture of
your feelings, feel into
your emotions - you will
hear a clear yes or no if
you enquire, 'does this
take me to feeling
better or worse?'
Confusion is unnecessary
when you choose to be
guided by only what
feels good to you.
Clarity is wonderful -
it's the divine clarion
YES in your body!*

SOUND IS LIGHT,
WATER IS LIGHT,

NECTAR IS LIGHT –
DRINK THE LIGHT FROM
YOUR INNER WELL –
ENJOY THE LIGHT OF
YOUR INNER BLISS.

Dream of tenderness

Tobias lifted his shirt. 'When I was a teenager I was living in another state to my mum, and I missed her a lot,' he said. 'See this scar? At fourteen I fell out of a tree onto some rocks. Mum flew to be with me in hospital. She was so calm, I felt like I was being held and yet it wasn't by her – it was as if a greater version of myself was holding me. Some years later I spoke to her about my perception and she smiled, "Oh my dear Tobias, I missed you too, all is well, you have grown strong. Life is a mystery to be enjoyed and shared. When I came to you, I meditated on you being purely who you truly are. I was really there to witness your self-initiation and even though you may not have realised it, I am always holding you tenderly and lightly."' Tobias finished his story and looked at Ti's feet: 'Would you like a foot massage?'

'Yes, please,' she sighed, lying back on the sofa.

Tobias sat massaging her feet, sensitively working with acupressure points to release tension. Ti began to deeply relax, tangibly surrendering, her eyes moistening with the sweetness of relief and being treated so respectfully. Through receiving genuine tenderness from another, she felt a warmth radiate from within her. The inner flame of liberty ignited by her surrender, her divine sacredness rose into her heart with the light of kindness and acceptance. Tobias yielded to her softness and became deeply entranced by her beauty; he witnessed her face and body shift, and a waterfall of freshness fall over her with every exhale. He had never experienced feeling so relaxed and present in this way with another person. Ti's heart began to flutter as she celebrated her whole being, and with pure energy releasing through her body with orgasmic ecstasy, she made exquisite sounds of release. She allowed the energy to move through her body; they breathed together as they EYE GAZED, sharing the blissful energy of liberation. Ti closed her eyes and went into a deep sleep, Tobias carried her to bed, leaving her peacefully resting and went home.

Ti woke in the morning to gentle music playing and smiled with appreciation, feeling deeply respected and understood.

✢

Let go of any personal inhibitions as you enjoy the song.

SONG: 'OPEN UP YOUR HEART' (FEAT. MOOJI & MATIA KALLI), MOSE AND SAM GARRETT.

Equilibrium leads to harmony

Ti arranged to meet Tobias at his mother's home where he was staying. Ava's home was very welcoming, a beautifully curated space with lush gardens, wide verandahs and a uniquely decorated abode.

When Ti arrived there was soulful music coming through an open window; it was the same song she had woken to the morning after Tobias had visited. Ti knocked gently on the door and heard soft footsteps.

Tobias opened the door, very happy to see her. 'Hello Ti, please come in.'

Slipping shoes off she followed him down the hallway, and noticing a half-packed open suitcase on a bed, enquired: 'Are you still arriving or about to leave?'

Tobias stopped, gesturing her into a large opulent living space. 'The latter,' he replied.

Ti sat down on large floor cushions. 'When are you leaving?'

'Tomorrow, I'm flying back home for a week before I fly to India,' said Tobias, sitting beside Ti who was looking bewildered.

Tobias softly smiled. 'I planned this journey to the HIMALAYAS long ago. I will meet up with mum, hang out with her, then travel on my own through the mountains. I'll be home in about a year,' he paused sensitive to her innocence. 'I always keep the promises I make to myself and I made this promise with clear intentions. I love the freedom that comes through embracing different experiences. I have been inspired by many individuals by their example to fully enjoy life and of course Joseph Campbell's great advice: *Follow your bliss*.'

Ti smiled and agreed: 'Hmm, something I read recently resonates with what you've said. Lust becomes dust, yet passion is the song of eternal lovers who live free from the beliefs and choices of others.' Ti paused, warmly smiling. 'I really appreciate meeting you Tobias.'

✛

Write a passage of praise in your journal for someone you've encountered who expanded your sense of self and gave an opportunity for personal expansion.

SONG: 'LIGHT OF YOUR GRACE' (LIVE AT MONTE SAHAJA), MOLLIE MENDOZA AND SAM GARRETT.

HARMONY IS NOT SOMETHING
THAT CAN BE FORCED.
HARMONY IS AN EXPERIENCE
OF ALLOWING EVERYTHING TO
FALL INTO PLACE.
HARMONY IS BEYOND
TIME AND SPACE.

White Tara Mantra

Blessings for Longevity

oṃ tāre tuttāre
ture mama āyuḥ-puṇya-jñāna-
puṣṭiṃ kuru svāhā

The Valorians

Imagine this archetype rising within our culture and self-enquire if you are called to explore and embody any aspect.

✧

The idea of death has no power over these enthusiastic souls, despite what they have been asked to believe, they know they are made from timelessness and are not bound to any mental limitation.

Valorians uphold a strong desire to be fully alive and choose to flow with life, guided by the knowing of their own destiny, rhythmic intelligence of their heart and passionate essence held deep within the centre of every cell. They are deeply inspired by beautiful music, and feeling natural and harmonic sounds at a cellular level, they love to move their body freely in celebration of just being alive.

Valorians have surrendered any resistance to inner harmony and happiness, giving rise to joyous thanksgiving for their life and everything they encounter.

Through harmonious self-communion they experience continuous evolution, their DNA portals fully open to sacred human beauty and higher states of unity. They understand that to limit or diminish others is to do the same to themselves.

Valorians are very allowing and nothing disturbs their inner harmony as they focus upon softly singing paradise into being. The sound of their voice soothes, uplifts, liberates, calms and inspires. They use their voice very kindly, understanding the power of their humanity and respecting their ability to shift perception. They speak with a soft touch and a fragrant warmth that invites the heart to open and the eyes to close. Their voice dispels curses and any negative self-talk, activating and liberating deeply coveted true heart desires in others. When they speak, doors open, armourr around the heart dissolves and songs of love are sung.

———

SONG: 'WHITE TARA MANTRA', RINZIN WANGMO.

Gayatri Mantra
Om Bhuur-Bhuvah Svah
Tat-Savitur-Varennyam
Bhargo Devasya Dhiimahi
Dhiyo Yo Nah Pracodayaat

✣

Meditate with this mantra,
burn away all blocks and
fears with the sounds of
purity, surrendering any
resistance to liberty through
your divine will, ensuring all
intentions and actions come
from the heart.

✣

Many blessings for a life
filled with grace, harmony,
unity, beauty, love and joy.

✣

Place your hands on your
throat, on your ears and your
lips and offer yourself a
genuine, warm smile.

SONG: 'GAYATRI MANTRA'.
ALBUM: *GALIM*, LEMON AND SOUL & OR
MAHAPATRA.

Appreciation is my hammock

I am profoundly relaxed,
I swing gently with appreciation,
supported by my own good will.
As I am softly present,
I receive so much more than I imagined possible.
I am awake, I am aware, I am relaxed.
I am in love with life, boundlessly content,
I am filled with joy, it's always the right time to be alive.
I am blissful, intoxicated by inner my divine grace.
I trust my essence,
the fragrance of eternal life that guides me,
I can taste the sweetness,
I can hear the love song,
I can touch the air moving through open portals,
I breathe and fearlessly allow.
I can easily feel what is a yes.
I can clearly see so much to appreciate everywhere.
My life is simple, clean, honest -
nothing fake, nothing pushed, nothing forced,
I find softness wherever I am.
I find interdependence self-supporting,
I say yes to getting in the lifestream.
I effortlessly float downstream,
carried by one 'yes' after the other,
towards what I am truly wanting.
I always stop and smell the roses, touch the air,
listen to birds, watch insects, enjoy all weather.
I always say thank you, thank you, thank you.
I joyously appreciate my life, such joy, love and bliss!
I unfurl my nervous system to bloom with evolution,
I am well beyond the past now,
I shape shift into being present here and now.
I have let go of any self-repression.
I illuminate the future with enthusiastic appreciation.
I carry sacred human warmth forward into the future.

Entering THE HEART of paradise

You touch everything
with your whole being -
contemplate your soft, subtle touch.
How do you touch others -
with your singing eyes,
your listening ears,
your relaxed mouth,
your caressing fingers,
your sensual body as it moves,
your gossamer hair,
your light, open mind and
the rose upon your heart?
Your touch is everlasting,
it brings ripples of future dreams
into now,
gently moving nourishing mists,
sprinkling glitter
across the turquoise ocean,
scattering stars
through the night sky,
opening new flowers
and swaying the trees
in paradise.
Beauty is in the heart
of the beholder.

Dream of forgiveness

As you enter these dreamscapes, follow Ti deeper into the valley of the open heart. Invite yourself to receive the GOLDEN TOUCH of compassion, forgiveness, freshness, creativity, love and joy.

÷

Ti drove to visit her oldest sister Cheri who lived high in the mountains, as she reached the last part of the journey the unsealed, winding roads slowed her down. Ti opened her window and was immediately greeted with the fragrance of the lush forest and bird's song through the gullies.

Cheri welcomed Ti at the retreat entrance and led the way to her studio home. 'Sit down darling heart, take a moment for yourself, would you like a chai?' she enquired.

'Yes thank you,' Ti nodded, as she relaxed on the large day bed.

Cheri brought chai in and as she sat down with Ti, she said, 'You look different sweetheart, you look refreshingly present.'

'Hmm yes, life has brought some ... I have been ... actually, I cannot describe what is happening.' Ti spoke quietly, in between sipping her chai. Cheri smiled softly and gazed gently at Ti over the rim of her cup. Ti continued: 'I am beginning to understand that I am not a victim of circumstance. I am really starting to comprehend how I am creating my own experiences.' Cheri ever so slightly raised an eyebrow and Ti continued: 'You did see that I thought I was a victim, I know that you did, and I thank you for trusting I'd work this out. I am truly sorry for my impatience last time I saw you.'

'It's forgiven Ti, I know your reaction was not about me. I'm so grateful that you are giving yourself space to learn and grow – go gently darling, let it all go. The past really doesn't matter, this day is golden. Would you like me to give you a head and face massage?'

'Oh yes please, that would be wonderful!' accepted Ti.

Cheri ushered her to a prepared therapy room. Ti lay down and closed her eyes, heart full of gratitude and appreciation, eyes moistening with sweet acceptance. When Cheri finished working on Ti, she put flowers in her hair and kissed her warmly on the cheek.

SONG: 'A THOUSAND SUNS', GURU GANESHA BAND AND PALOMA DEVI.

WE COME TOGETHER
IN LOVE FOR PEACE,
WE CREATIVELY BUILD
NEW STRUCTURES
AND SHARED MORALS
THAT ARE MORE
COMPASSIONATE
AND LESS
DESTRUCTIVE
AS WE SPIRITUALLY
MATURE.

Dreams of touching emptiness

That evening Ti sat in the gardens with Cheri. 'This is such a sacred space,' she said, looking around in awe. 'It is more beautiful every time I visit. What could be more satisfying than creating such beauty?'

'War,' replied Cheri.

'No!' exclaimed Ti in disbelief.

'To those that repress their hearts, war can be a very satisfying display of power for the disempowered. High levels of inner conflict create a focus towards winning a battle or control over free energy and creative spirits, especially to those who feel victim to their emotions. That's why I am serious when I say don't take things too seriously,' Cheri laughed. 'I have some good news to share – I have accepted an invitation to paint murals and work on the gardens at The Beloved's Temple in the Himalayas – a wonderful journey of personal enrichment.'

'Wow, that's great news, when do you go?' enquired Ti.

'In a week,' replied Cheri, casually adding, 'I'll be away for the rest of the year.'

Ti paused, just breathing, welcoming the embrace of grace as she allowed her feelings around Cheri leaving to settle with thoughts founded in generosity.

'Would you like to stay here while I am gone?' Cheri continued. 'You could also use my studio for your work, all rent free.'

Taking a moment to process, Ti realised that this was more than she'd been dreaming of. 'That would be quite amazing. I really want to move out of my noisy apartment before the lease renewal and, oh my goodness, without rent I could work just on my collection and commissions.'

'Ah, wonderful,' rejoiced Cheri, 'and I am so happy that I will be in the Himalayas with Ava. You remember Ava, my friend?'

'Yes,' replied Ti biting her lip, 'I met Tobias.'

'Ooh la la,' replied Cheri, 'he's pretty special.'

'Unforgettable,' replied Ti looking around the garden, as she privately enjoyed contemplating him and their encounter.

+

Visit beautiful gardens and practise the art of truly letting go of all fears.

Star mothers' dream

Cheri and Ti walked around the property in the morning before Ti headed back to the coast. In a hallway Ti stopped Cheri as she admired a couple of paintings hanging on the wall. 'These are new! I love them! Could you please tell me the story that goes with them?'

'You remind me of your eight year old self when you get excited like this,' Cheri smiled. 'It's actually very sweet, I love your openness.' She pointed to the painting with a yellow star. 'This one is about the star mothers, the ancient women who held the clarity, self-confidence and devotion needed to guide human evolution. They took it upon themselves to cultivate a safe container for increasing the spirit of consciousness. My understanding is that we evolve through many thousands of water births until we realise we must free ourselves from repeating patterns as they no longer serve our evolution. The paradox of the star mothers is that they created patterns for our wellbeing, which at some point we must let go of to grow beyond and evolve. As I painted the star mothers they spoke through my heart.'

'What did they say?' enquired Ti.

'First to let go of the past, have courage to create anew with heart-led intuition just as they did. We come through many different portals to experience the sacredness of our humanity. They say we are each starseeds and through our imaginations we can illuminate our multidimensionality, we just need to ask the right questions to our sacred heart,' Cheri laughed. 'The white peacock is for endless blessings, the mer-people to honour the oceans from which we have come and the kookaburra a reminder not to take anything too seriously.'

✢

Look into this painting, is there a vision or story that comes to you? Journal any creative musings. If you feel inspired explore painting one of your own dream stories on wood.

SONG: 'WATER AND SKY', AJEET AND SAM GARRETT.

166

Dream
into the mystery

'I love this too, who is the woman in this painting?' enquired Ti.

Cheri looked at the painting for a while. 'I was inspired to create this painting after contemplating a young woman I travelled with through South America, her name was Melody. She was very sensuous, softly luminous and the corners of her mouth gently upturned as if she was quietly amused. She was very centred and relaxed, a mystery seemed to run deep through her being. At night she would gaze at the sky and sing these incredible otherworldly sounding love songs. She inspired me to more adventure and encouraged me to consider travelling to the Himalayas with her. Wherever we travelled, she intuitively discovered the most beautiful gardens.

'We were sharing a room in a tiny village near Lake Titicaca, and I woke up one morning to discover she was gone. On her bed was a bunch of red roses – there was no note – just the sweetly fragrant roses.

'She became a mystery to me and recently when I self-enquired about her I was shown a vision of her in a garden holding a rose to her heart. To understand this better, I began this painting. As I painted, spiritual mysteries I had contemplated for some time became illuminated. I perceived the vision was about the blooming of the rose upon the cross of matter which represents our eternal and unique nature. This opened up my understanding to the self-mastery of the spiritualisation of matter. Much of what I witnessed while staying at Amrita's temple has also unfolded into a joyful understanding. I understand that through devotion to embodying pure joy, appreciation and love the nectar of Amrita – renewal – may flow through every cell.'

'Oh, how beautiful!' exclaimed Ti.

÷

If you feel inspired explore the concept of the blooming of the rose upon the cross of matter; express this in any way that flows. Consider expressing this in a song, dance, full body massage, creating an altar, sewing, gardening, cooking, painting or writing.

———

SONG: 'SHIVOHAM' (LIVE) (FEAT. GURUGANESHA SINGH), SNATAM KAUR AND RAM DAS.

Dreams from heart
to hand to heart

Cheri guided Ti around the kitchen garden to gather kale, shiso, mint leaves, cucumber, lime and mulberries to put into their morning juice.

As they sat enjoying the refreshment, Ti smiled. 'I love your juices, they are so energising. I am saving to buy a juicer, so I am stoked I can use yours while I stay here.' Ti paused and continued enthusiastically: 'I have brought the latest piece in my collection with me in the hope that I could photograph you in it, would that be okay?'

Cheri replied, 'Absolutely, I love wearing your pieces, they make me feel like a goddess.'

Ti helped Cheri to put on the gossamer fine dress.

Cheri ran her hands over the intricate details in admiration. 'It fits me so well! Oh darling, you're so talented, there's nothing quite like your heart to hand pieces, full of love and joy, they're invaluable and incomparable – true gestures of your heart.'

Ti squealed with delight. 'Surprise, I made this in your size hoping you'd love it and could give the sample to you! I noticed you admiring a similar dress on one occasion which inspired me to create this design for my collection.'

'Oh Ti, I do love it very much, it is so fine and light, I could take it in my luggage.' Cheri began dancing around: 'Under the strawberry moon and twinkling stars high in the mountains I will dance in this heavenly dress.'

Joy and love together inspire a self-perpetuating creativity which we experience as real life ongoing.

Explore working with your hands to create gifts for friends, family and/or offerings and blessings to loved ones passed, the elementals, spirits and Gaia. As much as possible gather things from nature and creatively work them into a beautiful expression of appreciation with the golden touch of your heart energy moving through into your hands.

———

SONG: 'SHANTE ISHTA' (MOSE & RESUEÑO MIX), SUYANA.

The dissolving of taboos
that limit our individual
self-expression and
exploration into greater
love is a sacred offering,
it is time for humanity
to appreciate those who
honour true-self and
the evolutionary
forces of the divine.

Dream into the
heart of strength

Ti paused at an old photo on the living room table: 'This is beautiful, is this – no – is this my dad?'

Cheri paused considering how to begin before replying: 'Yes, it is actually.'

'How did you get this? Ti enquired. 'I have never seen it, it looks like him and yet, I have never seen photos of him when he was that young.'

'I innocently found it actually. When Tom was preparing to come back here from Vietnam, he sent some boxes of his belongings ahead. The boxes arrived and one of them was damaged. I spoke to Tom and he asked if I could check that everything was dry inside. I opened up the box, everything looked fine, and I came across this photo. I had the same reaction, I thought it looked like my stepdad and yet ... no, couldn't be ... and then I turned it over and read this,' Cheri turned the photo over.

Ti read slowly out loud: 'To my true love Tom, yours forever, however the wind blows, Kim.'

'I was perplexed by this,' Cheri responded, 'so I spoke directly to Tom when he returned. It was a very interesting conversation – he was very open, it blew all my preconceived ideas away. I was surprised at how I hadn't perceived any of what he told me. Anyway, long story short, Tom and Kim were once lovers, well before Kim and Jasmine met and fell in love. As my dad transitioned before I was born and Jasmine married Kim when I was about two, I never knew. All three of them are very at ease about their past connections, will happily answer any questions and only uphold appreciation for shared journeys.'

'Wow, that changes so much in all my perceptions,' Ti sat down with the photo in her hands.

Cheri sat next to her adding, 'This has shown me that true love is boundlessness, unpredictable and without prejudice.'

÷

Contemplate if anyone you know, including yourself, has been misunderstood. Place your hands over your heart and allow compassion to flow.

SONG: 'BABA HANUMAN'.
ALBUM: *SRI*, SHANTALA.

Dream into the heart of warmth

'I feel I am only beginning to properly relate to Mum, I have realised that I was projecting cultural archetypes onto her rather than understanding who she really is as an individual. I need to be more observant and giving,' said Ti humbly, still processing her innocence.

'Go gently with yourself Ti, we have each been living our best life – give yourself some space,' replied Cheri. 'We don't have to be perfect, nor do we have to have everything all figured out. Life only becomes complicated by judgmental thoughts, we have nothing to prove. Our true feelings about how much we love one another are worth listening to and quite simply if we choose to think and believe in a way that feels authentically good to us, continuing to believe in and grow our happiest dreams, everything flows without suffering.'

Ti reflected upon her parents and their connection to Tom. 'Goodness me, when I look back with this new perspective, I see how warm and loving towards one another they are, and very inclusive too. Tom is always welcomed and I presumed it was because he was your uncle and yet it is far more complex than that. They really do seem to love each other without binding or being held to the past.'

Cheri smiled: 'Yes, they certainly love each other with a deep appreciation and respect. They do not behave as though there is anything to hide; their inclusive warmth and humour is very disarming. They have shared much of their story with me but also said to me that it's not the whole story because all life is a never-ending love story.'

+

Listen to the song as you trace your fingers over a photograph of your own face, imagine all the untold love stories that are within you, imagine yourself as the new one emerging to live your own never-ending love story and through living this new story you will touch the hearts of many. Perceive yourself as a gift as you live authentically by your own heart.

SONG: 'TRYAMBAKAM' (FEAT. CHANDRA LACOMBE),
ALBUM: *MOTHER OF ALL (432HZ REMASTER)*, MANEESH DE MOOR.

Beloveds dream

Cheri walked Ti to her car, pausing to enjoy the view, 'This view reminds me of Kim and Jasmine. They wander through here every time they visit, holding hands as if they have never been here before, just exploring – they look so youthful. The light around them together has a beautiful soft green hue.' Cheri continued, smiling to herself, 'Green for kindness, for liberation and forgiveness, for joy, for happy, fresh beginnings.' Ti responded thoughtfully: 'I am inspired, I celebrate Kim and Jasmine, all that they've ever been and who they are becoming.'

Dear sweetest beloved,
We are most certainly a blessing to one other.
Our love knows no limit, it knows greater.
Our hearts are free, we touch lightly.
You are free, I am free.
We declare all free by our singing hearts.
Love is royal, love dissolves cold empires.
Love wanders unbound.
Bound feet freed,
closed fists into open palms.
Upon the first kiss our hearts agreed,
we made a pledge to be our true-selves.
Beloveds becoming known to the mystery,
freshly drenched in joy,
eternally free to be,
tingling with freshness.
Thank you,
thank you,
thank you.

If you feel inspired write a love letter which may or not be sent.

SONG: 'TENEMOS TODO'.
ALBUM: *LET IT BE SO*, PALOMA DEVI.

Seven lovers dream

After Ti left, Cheri sat down and wrote personal letters to each of her seven lovers. She knew it was time to let go, time for a different kind of adventure. Cheri never hid the truth from any of her lovers; she truly appreciated the carefree and light-hearted nature of those relationships.

Her sense of self-worth had been liberated by the softness and warmth of gently exploring connection and she felt ready to deeply explore intimacy with one individual – a sacred union through a committed agreement to journey together through and beyond time and space.

Cheri felt that experiencing a true sacred union was very rare and yet, the concept really excited her. She decided that she must be her own beloved first – becoming a match to attract what she was seeking. As she contemplated the idea and surrendered her imagination to refreshingly exquisite desires of boundless intimacy her body tingled and heart fluttered in delight.

Cheri went into the garden and upon seeing mushroom caps contemplated Tom's philosophy about the mycorrhizal network: how everything is absolutely inseparably connected, supported by something small enough to be at the centre of everything, yet far greater than we can imagine. That we all share nourishment and the essence of life, and how there is so much beauty and unity below the surface, upon earth, in heaven and through the golden light that weaves everything endlessly together.

Do you remember the joy that you are?
Do you understand you are free to be free?
Let what is arising within you touch every part of your being,
feel if it is a yes or a no.
Privately and personally offer your love freely with deep appreciation for
everything - remember we are all connected.

Contemplate if there are any relationships in your life that feel stagnant or disharmonious. Write a personal love letter of appreciation and letting go to that relationship and burn it in a small ceremonial fire infused with healing herbs or resin. This process of recapitulation releases old energy to the element of air, initiating a process of setting oneself free to begin again anew.

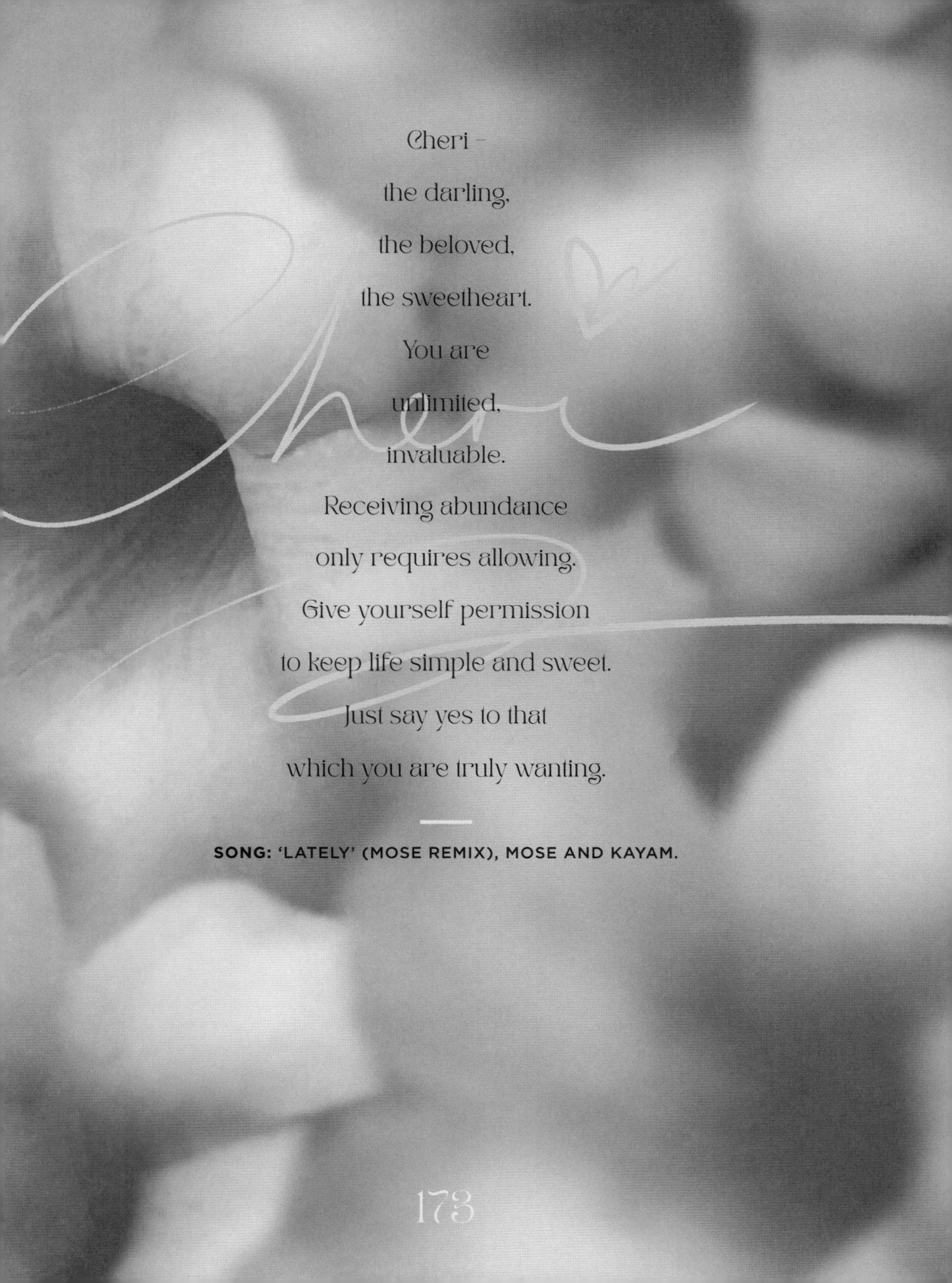

Cheri –

the darling,

the beloved,

the sweetheart.

You are

unlimited,

invaluable.

Receiving abundance

only requires allowing.

Give yourself permission

to keep life simple and sweet.

Just say yes to that

which you are truly wanting.

—

SONG: 'LATELY' (MOSE REMIX), MOSE AND KAYAM.

Dream of touching the sky

Cheri felt an amazing adventure ahead as she boarded the plane, trusting her inner guidance and paying attention to her finer feelings.

As the plane took off, she pulled her eye mask down and went into a deep meditation listening to Gaté Gaté, the heart sutra mantra. She guided her breath to the lower dantian; her mind followed as she imagined her lower dantian as a white luminescent pearl of incredible beauty – she welcomed energy from the heavens. She then focused upon her third eye in the upper dantian to perceive an indigo orb, and as she deeply relaxed the orb turned to green and a new love story flowed in a divine vision through her heart. She enjoyed every detail with great receptivity. As she whispered, 'I believe this to be true,' she saw herself standing at the top of a mountain as one thousand butterflies swirled around her.

Cheri smiled as she lifted her eye mask to see they were flying over the mountains and her heart began to quicken. The plane descended through soft clouds, touching down onto a land where ancient wisdom palaces are alive with devotion to the sacredness of a personal relationship with something greater and beautifully mystical. A land where the unknown is celebrated and all life is loved for its wild, intoxicating and glorious, true divine nature.

'Welcome to Gaia,' her heart sang.

Touch the sky with your heart,
say, 'thank you, thank you, thank you'.
Touch the earth with your heart,
say, 'thank you thank you thank you'.
Touch one another with your heart,
say, 'thank you, thank you, thank you!'
Liberated with strings of marigolds.
Joyous dancing, fragrance grows on trees,
sweet life is laughing with you.
You are the beloved, bow down at your own lotus feet.

Listen to the mantra in the song below – is there a dream that is touching your heart that you want to acknowledge? If so write a letter to self in your journal.

SONG: 'GATÉ GATÉ'.
ALBUM: *LOVE IS SPACE*, DEVA PREMAL.

The Amorians

Imagine this archetype rising within our culture and self-enquire
if you are called to explore and embody any aspect.

*Butterflies come and go - lovers of the seasons,
natural rhythm, flowers, flight and change.
Butterflies are a materialisation of the divine, free spirit.
Butterflies change light into delight.*

Amorians live beyond time and create space – love is space – they create more space wherever they go with delight, appreciation, love and the enthusiasm of free spirit. The space Amorians create brings a welcome relief from the illusionary pressure of time, not being or having enough.

Amorians prosper with life through the seasons, they are not bound to track and keep time. Their omnipresence is beyond time and yet they appear to have brilliant timing, showing up just at the right moment to lighten life, brighten perspective and bring the energy of light relief. They create delight just with their open and light-hearted presence.

Amorians are social butterflies: their laugh, smile and heart is boundlessly, endlessly light. They love to play with others, their touch is affectionately warm and sweetly delightful like butterfly kisses. Amorians will gently tickle the good vibes within one another to effortlessly release and flow forth positive energy.

With their joyful and inspiring presence, Amorians initiate a healing flood of love to flow through every cell as their presence entices the portals within the DNA of whomever they meet to open.

Love is effortlessness in its truest expression, the pressure to force or collapse comes from a conditioned perception of limited time and space. Amorians embody effortlessness as they are aligned with their natural abundance; they always have more love to give and so the quantum field responds in like.

*Love abound, unbound, stretch your wings and fly.
Be fully in love with life itself - appreciate everything.
It's natural to endlessly create with unlimited love.*

Butterfly kisses, flutter of
delight in my heart.
Golden space opening and
expanding around my body.
Butterflies emerging and transcending.
Self-love is space, space to
refresh, renew, emerge.
Beauty comes naturally through unfurling.
Beauty soars into life, life soars with beauty.
Trust, trust, trust.
Let go to the pleasure of joy,
delightfully free to be here now.

The butterfly meditation

We have a human tendency to gather the dross of self-judgement as we journey through life, yet we all have the opportunity to drop all disharmonious thought and thrive by simply enjoying life as it is.

Nourish your heart and set your spirit free by supporting your body's natural tendency to release all disharmonious energy and any tension that hinders wellbeing. When you practise the butterfly meditation, you are resting your mind down into the refuge of the calm centre of your body and simply allowing healing in the most profound ways.

For this meditation you may sit upright or enter a supported reclined butterfly, a well-known yoga pose. Whatever position you choose for this meditation, ensure you are very comfortable, well supported, can completely relax and let go of all tension as you breathe. The breath is simple: inhale through the nose and allow your lower abdomen to rise and upon the slow exhale through the nose, gently draw your lower abdomen back in towards the spine, keep the mind focused upon this task and continue in this way. As you relax, begin to imagine that with every exhale thousands of butterflies are released from your body – these butterflies represent any unwanted stresses. With each inhale imagine a warm golden sun glowing in your lower dantian. You may like to play nature sounds, a sound bath or song listed below. Meditate until you feel clear and calm with a gentle warmth radiating from the centre of the lower dantian. When you are finished open your eyes and sit with one hand on your heart and one on your lower dantian and offer yourself a genuine, warm smile.

SONG: 'TEMPLE OF SILENCE' (FEAT. ANNETTE CANTOR).
ALBUM: *GARDEN OF THE GODS*, DEUTER.

Beholding
THE GOLD
of paradise

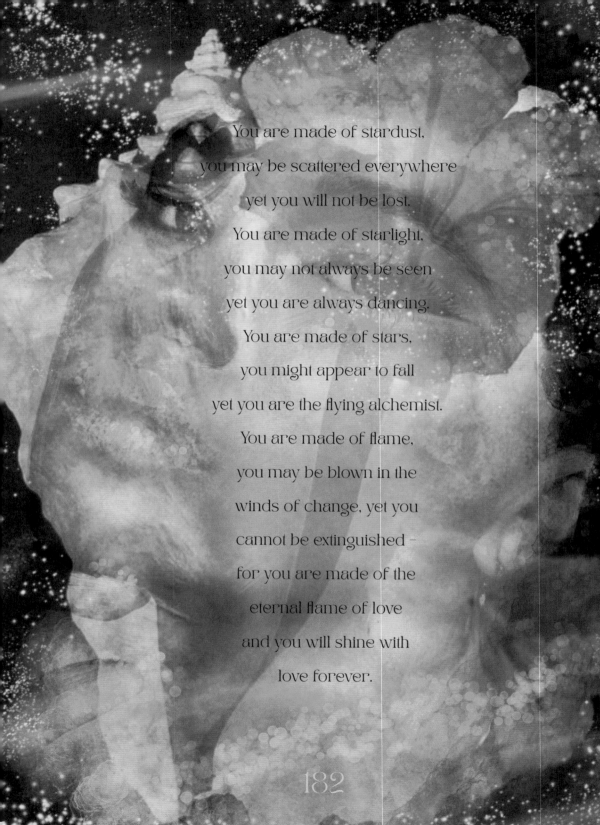

You are made of stardust,

you may be scattered everywhere

yet you will not be lost.

You are made of starlight,

you may not always be seen

yet you are always dancing.

You are made of stars,

you might appear to fall

yet you are the flying alchemist.

You are made of flame,

you may be blown in the

winds of change, yet you

cannot be extinguished –

for you are made of the

eternal flame of love

and you will shine with

love forever.

Seed of gold

To beloved Soleil,
Forever born of golden new light after winter solstice.
We loved you before you were born,
you were a star that sung to us as children,
you were a star that twinkled to us if we misbehaved,
you were the star that we wondered upon,
you were the star that we danced under,
you were the star that grew brighter when we met each other,
you were the star watching over our sacred union.
Thank you for inspiring us to create a beautiful world.
Thank you for sending us visions of your hopes and dreams.
Thank you for being very clear about what you wanted.
Thank you for trusting us to birth you into this life.
Thank you for staying centred as you entered the world.
We intended that you felt immediately loved and embraced.
We intended to allow you to show us your way.
We intended to be really good at listening to you.
We intended to witness your growth with great allowing.
We do not expect you to be a star on earth, you do not need
perform for us, you are free to be ever changing,
the small rock or the river,
the beetle or the leaf, the fairy or the secret garden,
the smiling cat sleeping or the warm sunshine,
the water nymph or the beautiful dragonfly.
Thank you for receiving the appreciation, respect and
freedom that we have given to you.
We loved you before you were born, you told us your name
before you came, what a miracle it is that you kept your
sweet promises and we kept ours. You are blessed by your
soulful intentions to appreciate all that you experience.
You are inspiration breathing.
Thank you, thank you, thank you.
With eternal love,
Papa and Mama.

184

Clearly defined liquid light dream

As you enter these dream stories, can you see the golden light moving through the words, the images and your mind? Can you see the gold of your true divine nature shining through everything you think, say and do? This is the realm of the solar plexus, the seat of personal power and truth, the subtle energy vortex central to the body vital for the realisation and actualisation of the true-self.

+

As Soleil sorted her belongings and packed for the move, she found the letter her parents had written to her when she was young. She sat on her bed and read it again, curious to see what new insights it would bring – each time she rediscovered it and reread it, her perception of what it meant expanded.

Soleil's parents wrote the letter for her seventh birthday, a poetic gesture in answer to enquiries as to why she deserved such a blessed life. They also spoke to her at great length about how abundance was not earned but came to those who saw the abundant goodness in everything. They encouraged her to grow her natural tendency to see opportunities in every challenge and appreciate what she had without any guilt or comparison.

Soleil had asked: 'But what about my friend Elise whose father died? She loved him very much.'

Her parents responded: 'You are always innocent as to why others experience life as they do. You are seeing them through your lens; you are not thinking their thoughts nor holding their beliefs. Don't worry about others and don't be distracted by another's suffering. Send them love and blessings, help them as best you can if they ask. Enjoy your own life without hesitation.'

+

Contemplate your own blessings, express them creatively in your journal.

SONG: 'CHATTR CHAKKR VARTEE'.
ALBUM: *FROM WITHIN*, NIRINJAN KAUR,
MATTHEW SCHOENING AND RAM DASS.

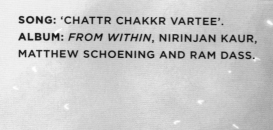

See with your heart in dreams

Love is not blind, love is boundlessness.
We cannot see when we sit outside of ourselves.
When we move into our very centre - our true existence -
clarity, confidence and kindness flow.
From our centre we are afforded a broad, spherical perspective
and can see that opposites are simply different
expressions of exactly the same subject.
Allow the true-self to choose what to focus upon.

Hot and dirty from packing boxes and cleaning, Soleil decided to have a shower. She thought it would also help to clear her mind, since she had mixed feelings about moving. Yet something in her was stirring, beckoning her to expand and dive into a new adventure – out of the familiar and into the unknown. She looked forward to living with more nature surrounding her; she knew it would suit her better than inner city living. When she spent quiet time alone, especially walking in nature, her heart kept showing her visions of her with her beloved, creating sacred spaces in their new home and travelling to places of great beauty together.

Just as Soleil got dressed, her father rang asking her over for refreshments. She happily accepted the invitation – appreciating how he seemed to know just what she was wanting. She found his company very calming, grounding, warm and vibrant.

Soleil always chose the longer scenic route to her parents' home, preferring to travel slowly and enjoy the drive. As she pulled up to her parents' home, a clear and certain perspective came to her – life should be purely about life, about letting the creative spirit flow naturally. She decided to let go of the myths she had lived by; she wanted to adventure into a new territory of womanhood. She wondered what being a woman would feel like if one could dissolve all impressions of disempowerment – myths about taboos, princesses, queens, stepmothers and mothers. That would be a neutral androgynous state of being, clear of the past, liberated, she thought to herself.

✦

Recall any myths of female disempowerment you have heard; write them out on a piece of paper and release them by burning them in a ceremonial fire.

SONG: 'MAYRAY MEET GURDAYV'.
ALBUM: *A THOUSAND SUNS*, GURU GANESHA BAND AND PALOMA DEVI.

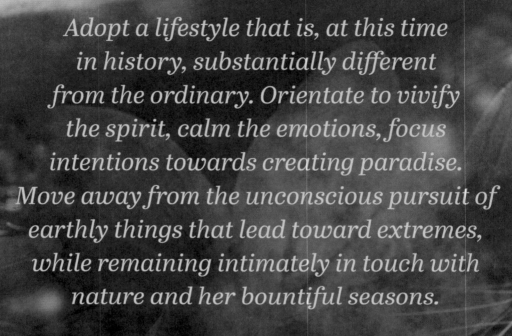

*Adopt a lifestyle that is, at this time
in history, substantially different
from the ordinary. Orientate to vivify
the spirit, calm the emotions, focus
intentions towards creating paradise.
Move away from the unconscious pursuit of
earthly things that lead toward extremes,
while remaining intimately in touch with
nature and her bountiful seasons.*

When different perspectives are offered a golden opportunity presents to attune to our core being, listen to 'gut' feelings and reflect upon our own truth. Defending your point of view is not self-empowering. When understanding or clarification is sort by others, relax, breathe and direct any positive self-beliefs into every cell of your body and allow your truth to permeate your surrounding energy field; from this place very little will need to be said. Our personal vibration speaks louder than our words.

Dream of golden truths

Kim welcomed Soleil with open arms and gave her a big hug. She squeezed him back and tickled him. 'When are you going to get some chubby love handles? Aren't you too old to be svelte?' Soleil joked, knowing her father honoured a daily practice that kept him mobile, strong and flexible. Kim laughed and pretended to try and lift her up: 'Oh no I can't do it.'

They sat in the courtyard, Kim had prepared some kombucha with jamu juice. 'Oh thank you, just what I needed!' said Soleil.

'So how are you going sweetheart? Are you excited for your move?'

Soleil motioned her head back and forth. 'Um, yes!' she replied.

'Looks like your friend the two-headed dragon has much to say on the subject,' observed Kim.

Soleil laughed, acknowledging she'd let her mind have too much to say, when she was essentially excited. 'Any advice for living together?'

'Hmm, sleep by yourself, sleep is for rest and renewal. I believe making love and true intimacy is best experienced when fully awake. You have two big bedrooms in your lovely, new place,' replied Kim.

Soleil sighed. 'But maybe we will ... well perhaps we might want the room for ...' she hesitated, 'actually, I'm not ready to start a family. Ahhh that's a relief, I said it, it feels good to admit this out loud.'

Kim sat looking at Soleil with warm eyes, offering space for more honesty. After a while, he spoke. 'Jasmine and I really knew that we wanted to have children together, clear as sunshine. I believe it's important to give yourself space to grow and feel into your truths. We are deeply programmed to reproduce, but this path is not correct for everyone. Now's your time to become who you truly are. We are living in very different times darling – incredibly expansive changes are coming. I suggest you and Joe sleep in separate rooms so that your relationship thrives without entanglement. It's wonderful to wake up refreshed, clear and present for yourself first. Go slowly, experience more life, cultivate intimacy together as you share what you truly value and learn to express love through sacred union.'

Dreams of bathing
in soul warmth

The next day Soleil went to the beach, giving herself plenty of time soaking in her true feelings and processing realisations as she reflected on her father's advice. She agreed that healthy relationships begin with clear communication, nothing familiar, no complacency and definitely no assumption or assertion. She realised that her beloved Joe had never talked about having a family. It was something Soleil had assumed was inevitable and, even though she no real desire to be a parent, was unconsciously expecting herself to step into that role. In the clear light of day, Soleil could feel that many of her beliefs about how a couple should live were highly influenced by culture, past and present.

It felt exciting when Joe and she talked about creating a home together with their complementary yet unique personal styles. Joe often said that by combining their different skills they could make their home a temple of real love. He wanted to build some furniture and agreed with Soleil's vision for creating an art studio so she could work from home. All in all she felt that there was so much to receive and look forward to. She promised herself to truly enjoy and appreciate their relationship and be mindfully present as her true-self upon their shared creative journey. She knew that her feelings were a precious guidance system and didn't need to over-complicate the delicate unfurling of their relationship by over-thinking. Deep in the core of her being she knew life to be an incredibly mysterious, holographically unique experience of sacred aliveness.

✣

In your creative journal open to a new double page spread and write across the top: *I know who I am in truth*. Put a decorative border around this spread as you contemplate your personal truth. When you are inspired with clarity of purpose and truth, express this creatively in writing or art. If you like the idea of this practice, extend it into a mood board or allocate more pages to this creative self-expression.

SONG: 'EARTH' (REY&KJAVIK VERSION), MOGLI AND REY&KJAVIK.

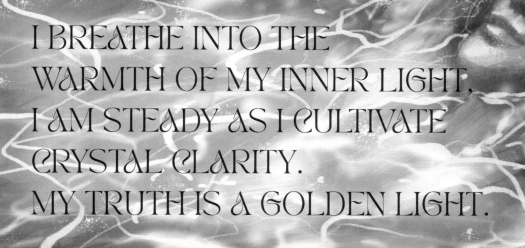

I BREATHE INTO THE WARMTH OF MY INNER LIGHT, I AM STEADY AS I CULTIVATE CRYSTAL CLARITY. MY TRUTH IS A GOLDEN LIGHT.

From the warmth of my heart comes reassurance,
from the core of my being comes clarity,
sunlight in clear water, warm sunlight upon my skin,
clear water moving through me,
clear water cleansing and refreshing my perspective.
I know who I am in truth, I know adventure calls me,
I embrace knowing clearly what I want from the unlimited.

Dreams of cherishing freedom

In the late afternoon after sunbathing, Soleil returned to the water; it had become very still, the waves gently undulating the surface. She took a deep dive and swam to the surface to enjoy floating as the sunlight kissed her face. She remembered the story her father told over and over again at her request when she was young. It was the story of the dragonfly's magical and mysterious journey to becoming an exquisite, delicate creature, free to fly in any direction it chose. How it began life as a water nymph, swimming around in the dark, murky water at the bottom of the pond, but something inside of it said to move towards the light. As it swims towards the light, it has no idea of who it really is or what it might become. It takes the tiny creature a really long time to grow in strength to get near the surface. Then, like magic, a reed appears and a voice inside says to climb onto the reed, and even though it has never climbed before, it climbs the reed, until it comes out of the water into the sunlight. As sunlight touches its body its wings unfurl, drying in the sun. It realises the wings are beginning to lift it upwards and so it lets go of the reed. Hovering above the water, it looks down and upon seeing itself appreciates its own exquisite beauty. It doesn't doubt its deserving of the gift of freedom; it accepts the invitation to explore the world freely and rises up and into the unknown.

Treasure the journey, never wish to erase the past.
Letting go of past is about letting go of the old perspective.
What we may regret or deem useless will change
with the light of a different perspective.
Different angles of light highlight unseen truth and beauty.
If we behold our life's journey with appreciation we change our perspective
immediately, magic happens in the light of our own love.
Let go, let the magic happen, imagine if you discovered you could fly?

Read the piece above and enter a dream space. Imagine if you could fly above your life and travel in any direction you wanted. Imagine that golden light or glitter guides your journey. Journal any visions and inspiring insights.

SONG: 'DEELAHLI',
ALBUM: *OSTRICONI*, YEAHMAN & MINA SHANKHA.

Dream of transcendence

At the end of the day, Soleil had created a clear picture of her future self, not too far in the future, just in the coming weeks and months – she decided she felt much more aligned when she allowed herself to travel lightly. She set clear intentions to self-honour and ensure that she and Joe never became entangled in their relationship and evolved beyond what had been.

Dear beloved,
The sun is going to shine, it always does.
I am supported and it is not by you alone.
You are not my rock, I do not anchor to you.
I feel confident to love you boundlessly.
I feel confident to appreciate you timelessly.
And it feels good to lightly hold you
as that is how I enjoy holding myself.
I set myself free from limitation –
I am free –
You are free –
We are free.
If for one thousand suns I lost you at sea,
I trust that my open heart and joyous appreciation
of all that you are would draw you back to me.
Any time apart is as much a blessing
as time spent together.
The texture of your handsome beauty, and loving eyes is unforgettable.
Your strength and charisma grow as your heart opens wider each day.
I know myself and I know you from our differences.
I can feel you coming for miles as the essence of you is
connected to the essence of me.
May we live forever true,
Soleil.

If you feel inspired write a letter to a beloved, it may remain in your creative journal or you may decide to share what you deeply feel.

———

SONG: 'MIRANDO EL FUEGO'.
ALBUM: *CAMINO DE FLORES*, EL BÚHO.

To dear Soleil and Joe,
Behold as you make all things new.
We see the world and yet feeling preludes believing.
We hear the world and yet feeling preludes listening.
We touch the world and yet feeling preludes connection.
We smell the world and yet feeling preludes fragrance.
We know the world and yet feeling preludes knowing.
Our feelings clearly show without doing.
Our feelings are precious, personal pearls - never to be
overlooked or diminished by the sun of another.
Ignore the pressure to look for what is not for you.
Appreciate yourselves to appreciate each other.
Lovers who follow their own bliss meet in unexpected
serendipity – allow the dance to dance.
Our work is to enjoy the great mystery -
receiving the gifts of true presence
through the light of soul.
May you both love yourselves and one another
in all directions.

Kim.

Crystal dreams – everything is new under the sun

Soleil organised to meet Joe at the beach for a sunset picnic the week before they were to move into their new home.

She waited for him in their favourite place, laying out a beautiful late afternoon feast to share.

When Joe saw Soleil, he jogged excitedly across the sand, pulling her into his arms when he arrived. 'Hey babe, I'm so excited, I just got a new job offer, a much better opportunity for me, it blows me away how good things seem to come together!'

'Wonderful darling, serendipitous synchronicity,' laughed Soleil.

As they sat chatting and sharing the meal, Soleil realised that the best place for them to be together was the present moment – anything else was just a story in her mind and there were so many possibilities. She could deeply understand the joy of simply being present, to expect the unexpected didn't mean there was anything to be concerned about.

Soleil spoke softly from a place of inner calm as she looked warmly and directly into Joe's eyes: 'How do you feel about us each have our own bedrooms in the new place?'

Joe paused for a moment, feeling her pure intent and with her gentle, silent reassurance relaxed into his own inner calmness and self-knowing, 'I hadn't really actually thought about this as an option, yet I feel it would be a great way to start living together – it feels spacious and allowing. Thank you so much for offering this as an idea. I'm in agreement, let's make this part of the adventure of becoming a new we.'

+

While holding a very small crystal or grain of sand in the palm of your hand, muse over this concept: everything is within the smallest particle. If you are inspired creatively express your perception in your journal.

SONG: 'THE ALL SEEING'.
ALBUM: *SONGS FROM THE TREE OF LIGHT*, MANEESH DE MOOR.

Bejewelled dreams

When Soleil came home from grocery shopping she found Joe sitting in the art studio beside a large easel looking very pleased with himself. 'For you my love, this one is more sturdy than the first one I made for you,' he said.

'Oh my goodness, thank you so very much,' said Soleil, gently laughing. 'I really appreciated the first easel you made for me so much. I loved that you made it for me, so even though it wobbled, I was too grateful to be that bothered.' She walked around the easel, feeling it's strong frame and sturdy footing. 'You have surpassed yourself!' she declared breathing calmly into her lower dantian to maintain inner harmony and a gentle flow of energy to integrate her elevated feelings.

'Oh, that's just what I wanted to hear, it's such a pleasure to make things for you! I'll leave you to set up while I put away the groceries.' Joe left the room with a wink.

As Soleil picked up her latest canvas to put on the easel she noticed an envelope addressed to her, so she opened it and read it with great delight.

To my beloved Soleil,
You are an incredible artist,
I am excited to see what you will create next,
no pressure though, none at all, life is so good -
together we are golden and sunlight.
We have plenty of time and space to relax into becoming
who we truly are in this next phase of our life.

÷

I adore how you paint with your eyes,
listen with your fingers
and breathe sunshine into our life.
You glitter with genuine potential and
glow with pure devotion to original creativity,
thank you for being you,
Love always from Joe.

Contemplate 'if this were my dream I would ...' or enter a dream space through images or poems in this section and imagine a new life story for yourself.

SONG: 'ASTRAL DAWN', ADRIAN FREEDMAN, AYLA SCHAFER AND SUSIE RO.

The Solarians

Imagine this archetype rising within our culture and self-enquire
if you are called to explore and embody any aspect.

✛

Honest simplicity may not seem easy if we try to think how that might
be, yet when we surrender to the soft warmth of our sweet heart, we
effortlessly find ourselves in a paradise of our own creation – relaxing
and simply enjoying what natural life brings, patient and unbound.

Abundance, sun dance, empowered dance, entrance.

Solarians are nourished by sunlight and laughter, they are never hungry – everything is an intuitive adventure of gentle passion, enriched by deeply resting in the dynamic stillness found bathing in the light of one's essence – the pearls of life force within the lower dantian. Every day dawns with rebirthing to exquisite new truths and divine beauty.

Solarians welcome sunlight upon their skin, enjoying bathing in all sun rays. They don't subscribe to any fear of the natural world, to which they feel great affinity. They trust in their own body's natural ability to find harmony and wellbeing, knowing that deep relaxation and appreciative presence are highly beneficial to the flow of qi. Solarians never rush – they never avoid any situation; if something challenging presents, they enjoy the opportunity for refinement of their own auric field, setting clear boundaries and loving intentions.

Solarians never ever complain or commentate negatively upon what has happened, preferring to observe life with mild amusement and appreciation. They express themselves with wonderful belly laughter and their voice is infused with an inner smile and giggle. Their lightness of being and enthusiasm is highly contagious. In their company everything is gold plated with appreciation, the past and future look bright – shifting like a mirage on the horizon without specific details or need for concern – and the present moment is vivified and captures one's full attention.

We are alight by the fire of our warm happy hearts.
We are unstoppable in our warm kind appreciation.
Joy looks good, I will wear it today inside and out.

—

SONG: 'ILLUMINA'.
ALBUM: *MAGDALENA MARIPOSA*, BACHAN KAUR.

Soft fire birthing – rise, bloom, grow.
Imagine as Venus and her sisters witnessed
the evolutionary shifting of human
consciousness in the Aquarian Age, they
sent forth clean and luminous energy filled
with pure passion for those ready to
birth themselves anew.
As the clarifying cosmic energy swept
across the planet, a desire for beauty
and unity was deeply activated.
Artists found greater creativity through
every element, expressing only joyous
appreciation for life itself.
Rebellion and revolution were replaced
with unwavering natural presence
and empowered grace.
Brilliant love songs sung through air.
Lovers emerged open to transparent
genuine connection – unspoken unity.
The golden age of healing light relief.

SONG: 'IN THE SUNLIGHT'.
ALBUM: *THE SILENT AWAKENING*, TINA MALIA.

Golden light rises into the heart

I awaken to the sun of my inner world, I invite this portal
to open, healing and renewing all aspects of my being.
I am aligned with my essence, essential-self, true-self.
Every day I rebirth anew to the sunlight of life,
refreshed and revitalised from my night's reset.
Each day I exist in a golden luminosity of pure awareness
and continuous faith, where the truth I see lives in me.
I am Seer in grace beyond time and place.
I practise non-violence, I dissolve resistance to peace.
I am Seer as I rise above the pain and suffering,
I transform all with the truth of liberty
that exists within my pearl of being.
I am Seer in timelessness.
I am Seer in boundlessness.
I am Seer in beauty.
I am Seer in unity.
I am Seer in harmony.
I am Seer in exquisiteness.
I am Seer in bliss.
I surrender any holding on to
what has been, I am clarity breathing.
I am love, I am joy, I am bliss.
My sense of knowing who I am in truth
is brilliantly clear and luminously eternal.
The phoenix rises.

———

SONG: 'CALL OF THE WILD', CURAWAKA.

Surrender to
the sweetness
of paradise

You are prosperity - I am prosperity.
Drink, sip, savour.
You are delicious - I am delicious.
You are sweetness dripping,
a river of innocence.
Catch this fresh nectar as it pours through life.
Enter this sacred hour -
the ambrosia -
come with me beloved wildness
and taste the gold of life.
Lay down upon this mossy earth,
rest in your wonderland.
Beads of your nectar - moistening pearls -
glistening upon soft flesh breathing with bliss.
From the kitchen of my heavenly body
divine nectar flows as I have been nourished by
drinking the nectar from Gaia's garden of Eden.

⁙

At the altar of my blessed paradise:
I promise to show my joyous thanksgivings -
alchemising all of what I know, hear, touch and see
of HER – the beloved's true divine nature -
into food that celebrates all earthly goddesses,
made lovingly by heart to hand from
my kitchen of heaven upon earth.

———

SONG: 'ESTRELLA DEL ALBA'.
ALBUM: *ORCAS*, LULACRUZA.

Rain blessings dream

As you enter these dreamscapes, can you taste the golden nectar – the divine essence of the creative true-self? Can you surrender to your own dreams and liberate them to become a celebration for beloveds to enjoy?

✦

Ti was inspired by the rain – it had been wet for days and everything was lush and green and dripping with freshness. She worked with tiny beads and sequins beads, sewing them onto soft tulle in rows that evoked the pouring rain. Her creative juices flowing, she continued working, using gossamer fabric to form an ultra-fine dress. She pulled it onto her mannequin and handstitched everything together adding more beads all over the bodice; when she stood back and turned her creation around she was very pleased. She felt some mastering of the balance of play with refinement and application of skill – acknowledging the environment around her inspired balanced creativity.

Ti heard a car pull up and from the studio saw Tom get out of his car, dashing up the entrance steps in the pouring rain. Another car came up the driveway, and a woman got out also moving quickly through the rain to the entrance. Ti heard laughter and joyous hellos greeting Tom and the woman. Ti wondered who she was, becoming aware that the retreat centre was vibrantly alive with new guests and artists in residence.

She returned to her work, devoted to completing her collection and commissioned pieces for clients – she could now perceive how, with focus and consistency, her business could flourish. She felt really good about herself in not seeking others' attention for validation. She contemplated how meeting Tobias was a catalyst for cultivating a deep sense of self-worth and opening to the sweetness of new adventures.

✦

Tuning into your surroundings right now, write about the details in your journal – what do each of your senses notice? What is sweet about this environment? Contemplate the kind of environments that are personally conducive to your creativity. Do you have these kinds of spaces or would you like to create them?

SONG: 'AHORA'.
ALBUM: *IN THE REAL WORLD*, ALEX SERRA.

The river dream

The rain stopped and sun poured through the green foliage, steam rising from the earth. The fragrance of the jungle moved across the land in gentle mists, as Ti wandered around the gardens, enjoying the new growth and refreshed energy.

Entering the lotus pool courtyard she met Tom just as he finished filming a qigong class. 'Good morning, Ti' – he smiled warmly to her.

'Good morning, thank you for sharing your practice with me. The fluidity of the movement style you teach feels like moving through water. I am inspired to go deeper into my own practice now, it's amazing!'

'Thank you, that's great to know,' replied Tom softly. 'I've practised like this for many, many years – since Amrita blessed me with her kiss of bliss.'

'Did you meet Amrita at The Beloved's Temple?' Ti enquired.

Tom smiled. 'She came to me in a life-changing vision. I had been practising a very precise kriya yoga, pushing my body around with the mind, becoming bound up, my practice had become a struggle. One morning instead of my usual practice I went for a walk along the mountain river and ...' he laughed, 'I was blessed by falling in! The river was much stronger than me.

She carried me through the mountains with great flowing strength, and eventually I went under. As I let go of all struggle, in a euphoric dream I was lifted onto the river bank by Amrita as she kissed me; then she shared a vision of an ancient practice, moving with grace, calmness, steadiness and inner strength, standing on top of a mountain. The next day I climbed to the top of my local mountain just before dawn, meditating in stillness and gently breathing into a great warmth coming from my lower abdomen. As the sun rose I stood up and intuitively practised, making the forms Amrita had shared. After many years of adventure I eventually found myself at a monastery in Vietnam at a class for qigong. The teacher and I both laughed as it began, as we realised I had been practising the same forms for a long time – after that I became qigong teacher.

✣

Enter into a dream space listening to the song below. Imagine yourself floating effortlessly on a river – there is no struggle – flow with your river dream, relaxing and allowing any visions to come. Creatively communicate anything that inspires you about your river dream in your creative journal.

SONG: 'RUNNING RIVER', SOUNDS OF NATURE & NATIVE AMERICAN FLUTES.

Dream of intrigue

'And I am here to remind Tom not to take anything too seriously!' the woman who Ti saw the day before ran over to Tom and put a string of flowers around his neck. She looked towards Ti with a beaming smile and said: 'Hello, I'm Rita, pleased to meet you, you are Cheri's sister, yes?'

'Yes, I am, pleased to meet you,' replied Ti feeling stirred by the young woman's vibrant beauty.

Rita gave Ti a hug that felt strong, soft and effortlessly affectionate, then kissed her on the cheek. 'Pleased to meet you too!'

Rita turned to Tom. 'Okay, time for a ride!' She put her arms around his shoulders; he laughed, helping her as she jumped up. 'Come on, let's go driver, please take me to the kitchen!' Rita turned to Ti winking. 'When Tom and I were travelling together I refused to get a rickshaw driver as I thought it was inappropriate, and so Tom said okay, let me carry you for a bit, and I will tell you if it's fun or not. Well, he didn't take me very far but we had a lot of fun, so every now and again, I get a ride from Tom.'

Tom started moving. 'Okay, we're off, you're getting heavy – I think you've been eating too much chocolate,' he joked.

'Hey!' Rita giggled as they departed.

Ti stood for a moment watching them jiggle out of the garden, becoming aware she was lightly touching her cheek where Rita had kissed her.

⁘

Self-enquire: have you met anyone that you immediately resonated with, who left a sweet impression upon you? If you feel inspired creatively, express this through making something with your hands – food, artwork, a flower arrangement, an oil blend, a garden altar – or by playing music or writing poetry.

———

SONG: 'JAI RADHA MADHAV'.
ALBUM: *LOVE IS SPACE*, DEVA PREMAL.

If we can let go of all preconceived ideas about what love should look like - what joy should be dressed in - how sweetness might flow - we might discover magic in the unexpected and allow ourselves to enjoy life fully without any self-repression.

Dream of
pure pleasure

In the weeks that followed, the wet season fully arrived and the weather became hotter and wetter. Ceiling fans circulated the air day and night through the buildings and the daily general vibe became very relaxed.

Ti went to the dining hall to enjoy a breakfast from the tropical fruit platters while she worked, becoming entranced watching king parrots drinking from a water dish on the balcony.

'Can I join you?' Ti looked up upon hearing Rita's soft throaty voice.

'Certainly,' she smiled, beginning to move her sketches to one side.

'Oh, would it be okay if I looked at these? They look very beautiful. I am fascinated by your work – Cheri has told me of your fine creations,' Rita beamed.

Ti smiled. 'Yes, for sure,' she said, leaving them on the table. As Rita looked over them Ti asked, 'How long have you known Cheri?'

'Not that long, I don't know her very well. I met her last time I came to see Tom. I didn't stay very long but we got on really well, enjoying afternoon chai and chocolate together. Cheri makes the best chai.'

Ti added, 'And you make the best chocolate, I'm very slowly eating the chocolate you gave me.'

'Oh, don't eat it too slowly. I'd love to make you some more; I have a rose chocolate that I feel you would really enjoy.'

'Okay,' agreed Ti as they smiled at one another.

Rita pointed to a sketch. 'Could I commission you to make this for me?'

'Yes, I could – I could start making it in a few weeks.'

'No rush, I am going to be working here for quite a while – that would be wonderful,' Rita smiled warmly, looking straight into her eyes. Ti felt the sweetness of feeling pure and honest connection.

÷

In your creative journal, sketch or write to describe your ideal garment for celebrating your true-self. Make it as simple or lavish as you want. You may like to imagine it made from elements of nature like water or flowers and plants.

SONG: 'INNERBLOOM' (FEAT. TANNER FRUIT & CASSIE WILSON), WEIR.

I have four mothers,
I love them equally,
I respect them equally,
I dance with them every day.
I am devoted to embodying their elemental magic.
I am a unique expression of joy, love, beauty and unity.
I harmonise with creation energy every sunrise and sunset.
I let qi* flow, I let divine intelligence move my body.
I am shown the beauty way by every season.
I am the flow,
I am star juice from heaven,
I drop into my body with deep relaxation,
blending with my elemental mothers
without any resistance,
they know the way,
together we alchemically transform
everything to shimmering
liquid love.
Mother Earth
Mother Water
Mother Fire
Mother Air

*Qi is the most dynamic and immediate energy of the body. This unique energy results from the interaction of yin and yang into the life force energy that makes up and binds together all things in the universe. It is paradoxically, both everything and nothing, always before completion. It has substance that eternally shifts so it never is fully known but can be clearly felt and distributed with focused intention.

Dream of surrender

Their lovemaking began effortlessly as Ti began making Rita's dress, an innocent unfurling that felt natural and delicious. It felt so good to Ti that a little doubt crept into her mind: she questioned whether something that felt so good was taboo, yet when she was present with life all fears dispersed like mists of the mountain. As she mindfully orientated herself to be on the adventure, her thoughts lightened and she could enjoy every moment.

Rita was very relaxed, playful, centred, calm and trusting in the process of opening to something completely new. 'I'm discovering a whimsical world beyond my mind's edges as I allow my body's deep intelligence to dance with you,' shared Rita with Ti as they caressed one another.

As they explored the experience of intimate connection and went deeper into their own hearts, the softness of their sacred union opened a space for purity. One afternoon, they lay quietly together in the valley of their shared ecstasy feeling the nectar of life pulsing through their bodies. Ti closed her eyes and fell into a light sleep, dreaming she was on a canoe covered with flowers being carried on a river deep into a cave within a mountain. As she entered the cave she saw a young woman standing under a waterfall, bathing in the rushing water. The woman turned to her and smiled; stopping the canoe, she invited Ti to step out and join her. As they stood together under the water, the woman firmly held her hand, then she took Ti out of the water to sit with her in the sun.

She spoke softly in another language, yet Ti understood every word. 'Inside truth there is only harmony – let the ocean of your mind calm, let the essence of your light rise and guide you, follow your personal bliss, it's safe to relax.'

Ti woke gently to the sound of pouring rain.

Rita had left her a note – I left you to sleep and wake up as yourself. I truly appreciate you – you are a one of a kind, xoxo Rita.

Practise enjoying whatever holds mystery for you and surrendering to its purity.

———

SONG: 'HIGH PRIESTESS', YAIMA.

Dream of secret sweetness

Rita invited Ti to come with her into the garden just as the sun was rising, as she wanted to share a secret of sweetness with her. Ti happily agreed, wondering what that might be, meeting her in the ambrosia hour on the grassed terrace overlooking the mountains.

'Good morning beautiful woman,' greeted Rita, taking Ti's hand and kissing her on the cheek. 'Let's go to the flower terrace,' Rita led her down the stone steps to where flowers of all kinds grew together in a rambling garden facing the east.

As a light breeze preluded the sun beginning to rise over the mountain horizon, Rita pointed to the dew drops on the flowers. 'When the sun kisses the water I want you to collect the dew drops in this,' she held up a tiny violet Miron glass bottle. 'I believe the flower's dew is the sweetest essence of the mists of love which move through these mountains with the caress of eternity – a more potent elixir when activated by the first light of day. I would love for you to experience it for yourself. You can collect from one flower or a variety. Allow yourself to be guided – there are no rules.'

Ti's eyes lit up. It sounded wonderful and they proceeded to collect the dew in their own bottles.

'I usually drink this on the day I collect it, sometimes all at once. Other times I put it into the water I am drinking over the day,' Rita chatted as she continued collecting dew drops.

Ti sipped on the water and sat quietly to feel the subtle sweetness. Rita collected flowers in a basket for the meal she was going to prepare for Jasmine's visit and then sat with her enjoying the garden in the golden light.

+

If you feel inspired, go into a garden in the hour before sunrise and collect the morning dew from flowers as the first light of day enters the garden and touches everything with golden blessings.

SONG: 'FOLLOW THE HEART' (ACOUSTIC).
ALBUM: *CEREMONIA*, YAIMA.

Dream of sweet joy

Ti instinctively looked up to see her mother had arrived. 'Jasmine is here!' Ti called to Rita.

Rita looked up from arranging the food on the table. 'Perfect timing.'

Rita went with Ti to greet Jasmine and they immediately resonated. Sitting down together on the balcony Jasmine felt like she was renewing an established connection with Rita. 'It feels like Rita and I have known each other for some time! Tom was right, he told me it would be so.'

'You're speaking what I'm feeling Jasmine,' Rita laughed. 'Tom told me the same and I can only agree with him!'

Ti deeply appreciated how they were getting along and smiled at Jasmine. 'Would you like a garden elixir, picked from our garden with the addition of the flower dew we collected this morning? Rita has inspired me to work with flowers and use them in food; it's been an amazing journey of discovery with her.'

Rita winked at Ti.

Jasmine smiled warmly looking at them together. 'Yes, I would love some and this food looks incredible. Rita, perhaps you might consider visiting Mists on Heaven? I feel it would be wonderful if you could work with Rose and I to create a menu for the open season; you come highly recommended as an innovative plant-based chef. Tom has been raving about your skill for years. What a blessing you moved to the region.'

'Oh that sounds very appealing,' said Rita, nodding. 'Ti has told me much about that sacred place. I must admit I have had a reoccurring dream of creating an exquisite banquet to be held in a secluded temple garden. Perhaps it is to be so. I hadn't quite perceived where that place might be, yet I sense I am about discover that.'

If you are inspired, playfully create a plant-based meal infused with flowers and fresh seasonal food. Celebrate your creations by sharing with good friends.

SONG: 'MINIYAMBA'.
ALBUM: *SHIKA SHIKA – BOTANAS SERIES*, YEAHMAN.

Dream
of harmony

'I really appreciate the food growing in this lush region – it's quality is simply amazing – and as I specialise in creating seasonal, organic, regional food, I am in heaven,' said Rita as she brought out another dish. 'This is the last one I want you to experience; these are macadamia and schisandra berry caramel creams, each dusted with different powders, butterfly pea flower, rose flower and schisandra berry. Enjoy!'

Jasmine and Ti were enchanted with the vibrancy and incredible balance of flavour. Jasmine commented, 'There are really no words for this, except it is a heaven meets earth experience. How did you come up with the recipe?'

Rita smiled. 'Thank you! I adventure forth enthusiastically and playfully to realise my sweetest heart-dreams, creating food like this is one of them. Fortunately I am never held back by imagining what others might think, good, bad or otherwise. It's taken me some practice and I am so grateful to have cultivated the patience to keep refining until I have created the most harmonious sensory experience of what I initially imagined. I play with making the joy and love I feel for plants, nature and her elemental spirits into food!'

'Thank you, thank you, thank you,' said Ti, looking softly at Rita.

Ti walked with Jasmine to her car and as they said goodbye Ti felt a strong desire to tell Jasmine of her deeper relationship with Rita; she paused to breathe and consider this.

Jasmine smiled warmly at her daughter, lightly placing a finger on Ti's lips. 'I can see that you are truly happy and for that I am so very, very grateful. Enjoy every drop of sweetness in your life Ti ... never force your blooming nor share what is delicate and private before you feel ready. Allow yourself to unfurl and bloom naturally – that is more than enough for those that love you – to witness your blooming is a joy. I look forward to seeing you both again very soon. Ciao, ciao darling.'

Ti smiled deeply from inside to out. 'See you soon sweet woman, thank you.'

✢

If you feel inspired gather some high quality, organic ingredients typically used to make plant-based desserts and playfully experiment by adding edible flowers – fresh and dried powders.

Dream of flowing

Tom concluded teaching with a short talk: 'Entering into states of deep relaxation and being able to relax into the centre of any challenge is the key to a happy of life. We have been taught by the governing cultures for eons that high achievement and success come from putting oneself under pressure to perform better than anyone else, yet this kind of peak performance is often short lived and leads to decline, as stress eventually weakens the mind, body and spirit. For longevity and self-mastery we learn to first move energy with intention from a relaxed inner state of being before taking action. Through practising these classic qigong forms every day, you will increase mobility, flexibility and strength – mentally, physically and spiritually – inner harmony will bring you into deeply relaxed states of bliss and may lead to great accomplishment. My qigong master instructed: maintain an inner smile, live with inner calm, be generously spirited, smile and project a positive outlook from the moment you wake throughout all waking hours, grateful as you drift off to sleep. The wisest masters have said that life is not intended to be taken too seriously. We should be devoted to living with inner harmony, blessing everyone through compassionate presence and our relaxed human warmth. Qigong is a practice to move energy, to create relaxed warmth in the mind, body and spirit.'

Tom closed the practice, bowing his head. He turned off the camera and looked at Ti and Rita. 'Thank you for being part of this video; having you both practising alongside me while I teach brings beauty and grace.'

'You're very welcome. I really enjoyed that, such a beautiful class, thank you Tom,' said Ti with a warm hug.

'It was indeed, thank you darling Tom,' added Rita joining in.

As Tom left the courtyard, Rita and Ti began picking roses from the garden to place at the retreat altars and dining hall.

'We are blessed Ti,' said Rita as she caressed a soft yellow rose.

'Blessings are flowing through us, yes I agree,' sighed Ti enjoying the sunlight upon her face, taking a deep breath, enjoying the early morning fragrance and sweet bird songs.

✣

Let these dream stories fade into golden light. Relax and just be with yourself.

SONG: 'STARDUST' (MOSE REMIX).
ALBUM: *PORANGUÍ (MOSE REMIXES)*, PORAGANUI AND MOSE.

The sweet spirit of receiving

I trust that every challenge also holds an opportunity,
that any struggle to gain power is just a struggle with power,
feeling powerful or powerlessness offer resistance to flow,
I am empowered, which means I am a facilitator of energy,
my work is to work with energy, not to force the flow of energy.
I stand with two feet upon the earth,
knees slightly bent, relaxed, centred, arms by my side.
I take a deep breath in and exhale, ahhh,
thank you, thank you, thank you.
I give forth authentic, gentle appreciation,
I am positive in outlook and feel enthusiasm for potential.
I know good things are coming to me,
I know opportunities are coming to me,
I am open to receive with no aversion.

✛

As I uphold a centred relaxed stance,
I allow my spiritual essence to flow, I feel it move through my body
I place my right hand over my heart, left hand upon my lower dantian.
I relax and breathe, expanding the lower dantian with an inhale,
gently pulling in with an exhale, my lower abdomen rises and falls.
I am so happy to be here now.
I smile at my body, thank you for housing the eternal being that I am.

✛

I take a moment of clarity and silence for myself,
I think of absolutely nothing as I focus upon the lustrous pearl of
divine energy within my lower dantian,
with my breath I clear stagnancy from all internal palaces.

✛

I stretch my arms above my head, palms facing heaven.
I take a moment of clarity and silence for myself,
I send joyous appreciation to all,
I turn my palms down and slowly lower my hands to my lower dantian,
I face my palms towards my lower dantian.
I vow to practise a life of compassion, respect, love and kindness.
I vow to take good care of myself and flow with divine life.
My love, kindness and respect flows to everyone.
Life is sweet, I flow with the sweetness of life.

SONG: 'FOLLOW THE HEART',
ALBUM: *OVO*, YAIMA.

The Yinarians

Imagine this archetype rising within our culture and self-enquire if you are called to explore and embody any aspect.

+

Yinarians can easily perceive obvious dualistic differences in any experience, and choose to reside in a nuanced world, finely attuned to the subtle energy within everything. They work in particular with the free, pure energy held in the unknown field, abundantly available for all creative processes. To work with this potent power, they ensure that they have clear and calm energy flowing through their bodies, never allowing disturbance to their inner harmony.

Yinarians akin their inner world to river systems, understanding that their whole system will flourish if the inner rivers are running clear and moving with ease through the body circulating and distributing vital qi.

The Yinarians respect their need for rest, they sleep alone with a clear intention of undisturbed rest and renewal. They believe the three human treasures, shen*, jing** and qi to be very precious and live in such a way to regulate, protect and strengthen these aspects.

They massage their body every day, first dry brushing, then self-massaging with a light oil, moving any stagnant energy, working to relax their muscles and deep into the fascia. After showering, they practice qigong or tai qi at sunrise outdoors in nature, if the weather allows, or indoors with fresh air and a garden or nature view.

Yinarians are masters at the art of allowing, neither distracted or disturbed by any other's energy field, behaviour or beliefs – they flow with ease towards their own personal sweet bliss.

They generally enjoy a hydrating diet of fresh flowers, herbs, green leaves, vegetables and fruits, fresh spring water, humid air, and especially flower nectar and morning dew.

*Shen is known as the psyche or spirit in western culture. Shen is said to be the driving energy behind activities that take place in the mental, spiritual or creative planes. Moderately weak shen often manifests itself as anxiety, mild depression or chronic restlessness.
**Jing energy, also called essence, is the primordial energy unique to an individual that is passed to them at conception. This energy governs the developmental growth processes in the body and the rate and degree of determination of the body.

Relax like you mean it.
move gently, with graceful balance,
let the rivers of your body flow.
Inner harmony and wellbeing comes
when you let the body recalibrate
through deep relaxation.
Relaxation brings healing.
The body is life living, trust your body,
let it move and heal,
let your body lead you into blissful surrender,
let miracles come through you.
✢
We are entering the phase of living into the question,
what do we want to become?
We are collectively unfurling as we expand
into our sacred humanness,
our sovereign creationship
with self,
other
and the infinite unknown.
Let the holy trinity happen,
let the grail flow
from plenty of nothing
into plenty of everything
into expanded nothing
into expanded everything
and so on life goes,
no need for collapsing or force,
allow the torus to be a smooth operator.
Let go of what limits your imagination,
enjoy the sweetness of your own divine energy –
may it flow freely as you rebirth.

———

SONG: 'REBIRTH', YAIMA.

Bridging
heaven
to earth

Freshness is upon us,
jasmine has opened,
smell the sweetness.
Come, come! Be here now,
celebrations have begun,
the bees are buzzing,
the world is bursting,
come intoxicate your being,
liberate yourself!
This bliss is yours,
fragrance releasing.
Let your soul fly free
into paradise of your
own creation.

The golden fragrance of heaven flows freely to
earth through every divine inner portal.
The mists of love and joy she releases through her
divine surrendering create a mysterious
and delicate lasting golden impression.
Her signature fragrance awakens the dreamers to
the power of the warmth of their humanity.
Her unique fragrance – her sweet essence –
releases as she follows her own bliss.

✛

Paradise made real within your body illuminates
and activates evolutionary energy within others.
Relax deeply, enjoy the inner rose blooming upon
the cross of matter, become a crystalline bridge
between heaven and earth.

Flowers bloom in dreams

As you enter these dreamscapes may you be inspired to
bridge your own golden dreams into your daily life.

*Mother Water's daughters each have a unique signature,
a divinely fragrant, subtle creative energy made by their virtues.
Without force or struggle, hesitation or denial,
the daughters bloom like flowers just when the time is right.*

The heady fragrance of frangipanis trees in full bloom filled the air, and the flowers that had fallen from the heavily laden trees lay scattered like hundreds of stars upon the warm earth. The frangipanis blooming were a prelude to the rare orchids that would rise and open when the luminous mists of the mountains became golden as the air filled with magical cosmic dust released by the fungi.

Jasmine and Rose knew it was time to head to the mountains and open Mists on Heaven Hot Springs retreat for the season. They connected intuitively on an evening of an early summer new moon, discussing their plans and enthusiasm for what was to come. They agreed they were looking forward to the opportunity to liberate and celebrate their most intimate desires and enjoy the benefits of deep communion with the pure liquid light – the natural hot spring water that would flow from the mountain.

Jasmine collected Rose two days after, and they took the familiar winding drive up the mountain. As they went higher mists swept across the road slowing them down. They turned up a long driveway and stopped at tall decorative metal gates. Getting out to unlock them together, they enjoyed the fresh forest air.

Jasmine turned to Rose: 'I clearly remember when we first discovered this property, what a magical place, and how amazing we became the custodians.'

'Ahhh yes, it is an honour to be trusted to care for this sacred place, to enjoy its natural rhythms and blessings each time we enter,' Rose said, smiling.

+

Plan a day trip to a beautiful place in nature, treat your journey as a voyage of the mystic. For pure whimsy and delight, listen to your intuition and body signals, keep a look out for signs and synchronistic occurrences, be prepared to alter your route and be led to somewhere unexpectedly divine.

Make a road trip playlist from your favourite songs in this book.

Dream of divine will

Sophie always paused to enjoy the fragrance and beauty of flowers whenever she encountered them, a promise she'd made to herself and kept since she was seven years old.

One late summer day Sophie was playing with her cousins in a beautiful garden, when they were all called to lunch. Yet a strong voice within told her to sit and rest for a moment under the shade of a large magnolia tree. Sophie closed her eyes to smell the fragrance and immediately enjoyed a daydream of fairies who lived in the tree – they had elegant pink bodies and their fine shimmering wings fluttered as they flew in and out of tiny doors in the tree's trunk. Upon opening her eyes, she saw tiny silhouettes moving behind the sunlit magnolia flowers. It was an amazing moment of connection to the magical natural world that left a strong impression. She decided to keep her experience to herself that day, sensing it too precious for words. She made a promise to always pause, enjoy the fragrance of flowers and be open to magical experiences; her heart sung with her decision.

From that day forth Sophie began to commune with what she sensed was the elemental energy abounding in nature.

Sophie matured with a lightness of being, and through communion with the elementals, became a skilled botanist and perfumer amongst other things.

When Jasmine was a child she first met Sophie as one of her mother's friends. Jasmine was intrigued by Sophie, clearly perceiving her as a portal to the elemental realms of wisdom. As Jasmine grew older she noticed that Sophie was like her own mother in that she didn't appear to age. When Jasmine and Rose became the custodians of Mists on Heaven, Sophie came with wisdom and rituals to initiate them into the realms of the elementals towards creating their own eternal paradises.

As Sophie arrived for another season of magic at Mists on Heaven, Jasmine noticed her pausing to smell the roses on her way through the gardens.

÷

A noble promise made to self and kept is an incredibly empowering practice. Consider if there is any kind of whimsical communion with nature that you feel might be beneficial ongoing. Write this in your journal, make a promise to entertain this practice and sign and date this entry.

Dream of
eternal devotion

Daksha arrived bringing a charismatic energy of high devotion and appreciation – her aura pure and brilliant with these virtues. Daksha lived through a refined practice of holding steady in the present moment, grounded in its sacredness, devoted to embodying life's highest virtues.

She warmly greeted the women who had gathered to prepare and bless Mists on Heaven for the seasonal guests. They lingered together for long embraces and kisses, enjoying the warmth and fragrance of one another. Daksha stood aside with Jasmine and Rose, looking into one another's eyes. Then standing quietly together, they held hands with eyes closed, sharing heart visions for the opening ceremony, embracing inner harmony and warmth to seal their good intentions.

Daksha began walking the grounds, ensuring the paths were clear and all spirits honoured, then headed to the hot springs to listen the mountain. She sat by the still pool breathing slowly. With each inhale she could smell different notes in the perfume of the mountain, and with each breath out she released gratitude, joyful praise and appreciation through her heart. After a while water began to drip from the orchid covered rocks above the pool, and she opened her eyes to see the orchids had opened with the steam rising from the dripping water. Daksha bowed giving thanks to the mountain for releasing her magical warm waters for evolutionary healing and renewal.

The soft voices of more women arriving echoed through the valley, everyone sensing the prophesied Golden Age of great beauty, unity, harmony and everlasting peace had arrived. The fragrance of the mountain infused the surrounding mists with the energy of blessings and renewal.

Her water is in you, your water is in her.
There are two kinds of water: that which is to be cleared and
that which is for clearing, let her do the work -
she knows by the fragrance of your skin what you are needing for inner
harmony to create the fragrance of your own paradise.

Contemplate and journal: what are you devoted to today? What are you giving your attention to? What would you like to be devoted to tomorrow?

SONG: 'STILLNESS DANCING', MARINA RAYE.

Dreaming together
in continuum

Many fragrant flowers bloom from the seeds of Venus and her sisters, each
surpassing those initial dreams and desires for creating beauty and unity.

When she was eight years old Lily had known she would have two beautiful daughters. One summer evening she opened her bedroom window and was greeted by a fragrance she'd never experienced before. When she looked into the moonlit garden, she noticed a luminous glow above a water dish. She climbed out of her window and discovered dancing lights above the water, as she silently moved closer, the fragrance became stronger. Lily stood mesmerised watching the moving lights merge to create images; she saw herself with a daughter born in spring when the jasmine flowers were opening and with another daughter born when roses bloomed on a mid-summer's morning. When Lily woke in the morning she was in her bed, but she noticed the open window and recalled her waking dream of the previous night. From that morning she began communing with the dancing lights whenever they appeared, always preluded with a distinctive fragrance. Visions of her daughters became clearer with the years, and so after she met her life partner, she was completely at ease and ready to become the dream mother.

Jasmine was the first daughter to arrive, followed two years later by Rose. As Lily cared for her growing daughters, creating a beautiful family home and garden, she continued to commune with what she referred to as the crystalline elementals for guidance and inspiration to bridge her dreams into real life.

⁘

As Jasmine and Rose made their way to the retreat's tea house, they telepathically communicated. They were well practised at this artful style of communication and found it highly amusing; many often wondered what they were smiling about. Pausing at the lily garden they communed with their mother, who confirmed she would visit them at the end of the week.

⁘

If you have a loved one that is open to the idea, playfully explore telepathic communication with them. Treat this practice as a game, have fun seeing what dreams of creativity you can send and receive to each other through this mystical practice. Journal your experiences and keep practising if it excites you.

Dream of the eternal ceremony

Rose and Jasmine entered the tea house, the jade walls and copper decorative details looking as beautiful as they did when they first painted them. They opened the elegant wall screens on each side of the building to the view of large magnolia trees and wild orchids, a temple-style roof stretched wide over all sides offering shade and weather protection. They hung crimson velvet curtains either side of the openings, scattered embroidered floor cushions and lay down a thick handwoven rug. The fragrant mountain mists moving through the gardens stopped in curled swirls at the edges of the polished wooden decks that surrounded the building. Jasmine and Rose lit incense in every corner and lit one hundred candles at the altar.

'I feel like I have visited this place in a dream – sometimes I expect to see Green Tara sitting at the altar waiting for us to join her,' commented Jasmine.

Rose looked around the space. 'Yes, I know what you mean, it feels as though we have been performing this tea ceremony together for eons, and yet every time, it also feels like a new beginning.'

'Always before completion,' added Jasmine as she knelt on the floor to set up the tea ceremony on a low wooden table.

Rose boiled the water and poured it into the old teapot.

'Do you know where this teapot came from?' enquired Jasmine.

Rose laughed lightly looking at it. 'Actually I don't – it's perfect though isn't it? Everything is perfectly mysterious; I feel the elementals are working with us. I love how our mother taught us to enjoy not knowing everything and to appreciate everything that is.' Rose paused and smiled at Jasmine: 'It feels very special to be here with you darling.'

'And I feel the same to share this wonderful experience with you! Thank you dear, dear sister of the rose scented stars,' Jasmine agreed as she warmly hugged Rose.

✢

Enter a dreamscape with the intention to draw inspiration for any kind of ceremony that you could hold as a celebration of your life. If inspiration comes, write it out in your journal and plan to perform it in the near future.

SONG: 'LIQUID SILK', MARINA RAYE.

Dream of the eternal sanctuary

Jasmine and Rose walked up the path lined with blooming wild orchids to the sacred mountain hot springs. The sisters breathed in deeply feeling increasingly relaxed with every step, enjoying the benefits of the fragrant mountain: a unique alchemy of her crystalline energy, mineralised steams and mists, lush forest, fungi spores and exotic blooms.

They undressed and slowly entered the warm water. As they moved across the bathing pool, they felt the heat increase where the hot spring water now trickled continuously.

'I wonder how long the season will last this year. I felt profoundly different leading up to coming here, as if a new portal is opening and incredible changes are going to pour through me,' said Rose softly, as she lay back dipping her hair into the water.

'Yes, I understand what you are feeling; I felt this too, a stirring deep inside as if a part of my true divine nature is very gently becoming illuminated, an inner phosphorescence bringing incredibly subtle transformation. I have begun working deeply with this very soft inner light, imagining it flowing through my body, creating an incredible inner steam, a mist of love for purification and renewal,' reflected Jasmine.

The sisters were joined by the other women who had arrived for the opening. They bathed together in the hot springs until the early evening.

Just as they were moving to get out of the water, Rose looked at Jasmine and smiled.

Jasmine took a slow inhale and exhale and silently replied, 'I agree it is time.'

Rose smiled at Jasmine with gratitude, kissing her on the cheek, then slowly stepped out of the pool.

Relaxing is invaluable. Imagine with release of all tension,
new flowers bloom in faraway places, in worlds yet to be known,
impulsed and inspired by your embodied sacred beauty upon Gaia.

If you feel inspired take a long hot bath, add some bath salts or favourite scented potions. As you soak and relax, enter a dreamscape with the gentle intention of nurture and renewal. Simply enjoy.

SONG: 'THREADS OF LIFE'.
ALBUM: *SHEDDING TEARS*, BUDDHA'S LOUNGE.

Dream of unfurling

Jasmine went back to her villa and sent a message to her beloved Kim. He would be the first man to enter the sanctuary since she became a custodian.

He replied almost immediately, 'Yes, it would be an honour, my love. I will come tomorrow evening.'

Jasmine hadn't seen him for days, and became excited at the thought of bringing him to the mountain. He had always understood the sanctuary was sacred space that she and Rose held for women. He never demanded to be invited in and, with a strong masculine trust and clarity, held a gentle flame for an invitation to be nourished by the mountain and her sacred waters.

Later the next day with the mere thought of her eternal lover drawing closer, Jasmine could almost smell his skin, especially his neck. With visions of his smiling eyes and handsome physicality, her skin tingled with anticipated enjoyment of his strong hands and warm body.

Jasmine cleansed her mind and body with intuitive ritual: dry brushing, massaging her whole body with sesame oil, bathing and then massaging again with camellia oil mixed with the fragrance of jasmine, neroli, bergamot, sandalwood and vanilla. She slid a silk dress over her bare skin, adorned herself with gold jewellery and put fresh flowers in her hair.

Jasmine lit candles along the pathway to her villa and in her sacred spaces, scattered rose petals across her bed and lit incense of vanilla and frankincense. The moistness of her willing surrender drew fragrance from the air. The rare orchids unfurled into the softness of the sacred night.

Perfection is the earthiness of our being,
surrendered to the bliss of authenticity.
Elemental harmony happens through surrender.
The mind and body a temple and sanctuary for love -
love made real through honest joy and appreciation.
The body is a breathing pleasure -
give thanks always.

Treat your body and mind as a divine temple through carrying out a pleasurable ritual, infused with beautiful and delightful details.

—

SONG: 'GENTLE SEASON'.
ALBUM: *TAO OF HEALING*, DEAN EVENSON & LI XIANGTING.

Lover's dream

At the end of the day Kim went to the ocean, moved his body to flow with and cultivate qi, meditated, swam in the ocean to cleanse and after drying his body applied ambrette and sandalwood oils. He put on a fresh linen shirt and trousers, bowed to mother ocean, warmly smiling as he left.

When driving up to the mountain where the mists meet heaven, he could sense her subtle nature – shifting, releasing, opening. He knew they would meet each other anew, their individual essence would be clearer and unmistakably affirming of the sacred and harmonious nature of their relationship. Kim never dismissed any dream of actualising his own true divine nature, remaining steady and strong, ready to fully receive and to warmly give, trusting his grounded strength would activate her having complete trust in him, inviting her to softly open so they may go deeper together into self-actualising bliss.

When he reached the temple garden and slowly walked the candlelit steps Jasmine was there, standing at the top of the path watching him move exquisitely towards her. They began breathing in sync with each other and the mountain, inhaling appreciation, exhaling fragrant mists.

He lightly touched her arm as they met and she pulled him close, and their eyes lingered as they passionately kissed.

A soft luminous mist enfolded them, presenting a completely private space in which to slowly make love. Inhaling the subtlety of their newly refined patterns, inner portals opened like flowers with their shared bliss, and they eventually rested together in the joyous valley of their sacred union with grounded presence.

Kim leant over and they shared the lover's kiss of eternal life. 'Goodnight my beloved Jasmine.' He left Jasmine to sleep and walked through blooming orchids on the way to his villa. As he lay down to sleep, her fragrant nectar flowed through rivers of his body. He felt an incredible inner bloom of warmth and complete aliveness and gratefully enjoyed balance of mind, body and spirit.

⁜

Enter a dreamscape as if this was *your* lover's dream. Self-enquire: what is my dream story, what are the details? Can I bridge my lover's dream into real life?

SONG: 'CUÑAQ'.
ALBUM: *PACHAMANTRA VOL. I*, RAIO & SOPHIE SÔFRĒĒ.

255

The fragrance of the elementals

Without the elementals how could we exist?
I give thanks, I am deeply humbled
to realise that without the elementals
this physical realm would not be so.

✛

Crystalline energy,
breath of life,
holy fire,
sacred water,
fearless presence.

✛

Crystalline,
Air,
Fire,
Water,
Earth.

✛

I bow down to the five virtuous powers.
With deep reverence I ask the elementals for assistance,
to alchemise my highest virtues, to actualise my greatest purpose.
My sacred bliss is a unique elemental fragrance of my new life.
I commune with the elemental world
to embody my true divine nature.

SONG: 'NIENDO'.
ALBUM: *WHISPERS FROM THE SEVENTH SKY*, SARIEL ORENDA.

The Fleurians

Imagine this archetype rising within our culture and self-enquire if you are called to explore and embody any aspect.

✧

The Fleurians embody the highest virtues of humanity with incredible warmth, compassion and a golden presence that uplifts, calms and relaxes those around and beyond their field through all space and time.

At sunrise and sunset you will find Fleurians outdoors practising ancient forms of qigong, meditating, walking, singing, communing with the elementals and bowing in reverence to all life on immortal Gaia. They live aligned to Gaia's FIVE SEASONS and their own true divine nature.

Every day they gather flowers for their altars, personal adornment and home. They collect morning dew, fresh flowers, leaves and fruits from the garden for breaking the fast of the night. They enjoy a second nourishing meal before sunset of freshly picked vibrant, seasonal plant foods and floral teas.

As Fleurians continue to evolve, they refine the patterns and habits by which they live, and this divine creativity gives birth to a flowering of cosmic constellations into new fractal patterns, guiding all expressions of life to evolve.

Fleurians are adept at refining their emotions so that they only exude great human warmth, always finding equilibrium and inner harmony, paying no attention to any turbulent thoughts or outer disturbances.

The Fleurians ride the rainbow serpent energy into dreamscape through personally attuned practices in places of great natural beauty. They believe the purpose of their life is to bring back dreams which liberate all suffering and celebrate humanity, healing seven relative generations from the past and into the future. As physically immortal custodians of the human spirit, the Fleurians are loving guardians of the dreamers who are awakening.

✧

Contemplation: How would I think and act if my intent was to align with Gaia's dream and become physically immortal? What would my life be like if I consciously opened to my multi-dimensional true, divine nature and embodied crystalline energy? What does the spiritualisation of matter mean to me?

SONG: 'UNBOUND', IFTEKHARUL ANAM.

Blessings

I am the golden dreamer, I breathe my dreams alive.
My dreams may seem wild and far out of reach,
yet they are merely wild flowers growing in a faraway place,
I trust they will one day send their formed seeds to me
upon the winds of change and I will be ready
to tend to them to bloom in the garden of my heart.

✛

I am strong enough to be soft.
I am passionate enough to be grounded in truth.
I am humble enough to keep on learning.
I am warm enough to be truly beautiful.
I am fearless enough to never give up on my humanity.
I am a living innovation to humanity.
I am an inspiration to all those I meet.
I am invaluable in my relaxed evolution.
As I awaken, I choose to go forth, I don't turn back.
I allow the embrace of grace to carry me through the portals
that are opening within my creative consciousness.
I let go of the not-self and allow the true-self to flow.

✛

Thank you to my body, mind and spirit.
Thank you Gaia.
Thank you elementals.
Thank you good spirits, guides and masters.

✛

I embody the gift of warmth to free my spirit.
I embody the gift of love to set others free.
I embody the gift of joy to be truly present.
I embody the gift of bliss to celebrate all that I am
and all that you are and all life past, present and future.

✛

OM Tāre Tuttāre Ture Svāhā
OM Tāre Tuttāre Ture Svāhā
OM Tāre Tuttāre Ture Svāhā

✛

Om shanti, om shanti, om shanti,
peace, peace, peace.

———

SONG: 'TE NANDE' (MOSE REMIX EXTENDED), MOSE AND CURAWAKA

Acknowledgements

This work was created on the precious and sacred land of Bundjalung Nation. I honour and acknowledge the original custodians of this land, the Minjungbal people. I live in gratitude with the omnipresent wisdom and guidance of Spirit. I pay respects to the sacred elders: past, present and emerging. With gratitude, I acknowledge the unwavering support of my beloved, Aaron Wilson, the love, joy, inspiration and wisdom of my daughters, family and spiritual teachers.

Resources

Akal Pritam – akalpritam.com
Akal Pritam Tatau, Creating Paradise Playlist – Youtube music
Tao Te Ching – Lao Tzu, translated by John H. McDonald
Human Design – Ra Uru Hu – ihdschool.com
Gene Keys – Richard Rudd – genekeys.com
The published works of Robert Coon – earthchakras.org
Thich Man Tue (Br Insight) Qigong meditation Youtube.
Heather Ensworth – Heather Ensworth Youtube + risingmoonhealingcenter.com
Adam Elenbaas – Adam Elenbaas Youtube + nightlightastrology.com
Channi Nicholas – Channi Nicholas Youtube + chaninicholas.com
Veda Austin – vedaaustin.com
Chucho Tresvida Ruiz – Swimming through the void Youtube + swimmingthroughthevoid.com
Pam Gregory Astrologer – Pam Gregory Official YouTube
Galactic Astrology – Galactic Astrology Youtube

About Akal Pritam

Akal Pritam Tatau is a mystic and naturalist devoted to the embodiment of personal bliss. A seer and illuminator working in the field of the healing arts to inspire and activate individual and collective potential.

A degree in communication eventually led Akal Pritam to working in publishing after a career as a creative director in the advertising industry for over a decade.

With reorientation of life after starting a family Akal Pritam became an internationally published, prolific creator of unique books, inspiration cards and journals, lovingly and specifically designed as tools to encourage following personal bliss.

Akal Pritam and her life partner reside in the Northern Rivers region of Australia where they make joy and love real as they follow their bliss.

Akal Pritam lives by the mantras: 'I am grateful for my life' and 'I am becoming who I am.'

AKALPRITAM.COM